KU-464-485

THE ENCYCLOPEDIA OF
Woodworking
TECHNIQUES

Jeremy Broun

Search Press

A QUARTO BOOK

This edition published in 2018 by
Search Press
Wellwood
North Farm Road
Tunbridge Wells
Kent TN2 3DR

Previously published as
*The Encyclopedia of Woodworking
Techniques* in 1993 and 2003.

Copyright © 1993, 2003 & 2018
Quarto Publishing plc
an imprint of The Quarto Group

All rights reserved. No part of this
publication may be reproduced, stored
in a retrieval system or transmitted in
any form or by any means, electronic,
mechanical, photocopying, recording or
otherwise, without the written consent
of the copyright holder.

ISBN: 978-1-78221-647-6

Conceived, edited and designed by
Quarto Publishing
an imprint of The Quarto Group
The Old Brewery
6 Blundell Street
London N7 9BH
www.quartoknows.com

QUAR: EWDN

Editor & designer: Michelle Pickering
Picture researcher: Susannah Jayes
Editorial assistant: Cassie Lawrence
Publisher: Samantha Warrington

Publisher's note
Woodworking can be dangerous. Both
hand and power tools can quickly sever
nerves, tendons or limbs with disastrous
results. Always exercise extreme caution.
Always read the instruction manuals
and use the safety guards provided;
for the purposes of photography, many
of the guards were removed – it is not a
recommended procedure. As far as the
methods and techniques mentioned in
this book are concerned, all statements,
information and advice given here
are believed to be true and accurate.
However, neither the author, copyright
holder nor the publisher can accept any
legal liability for errors or omissions.

Printed in China

MIX
Paper from
responsible sources
FSC® C101537

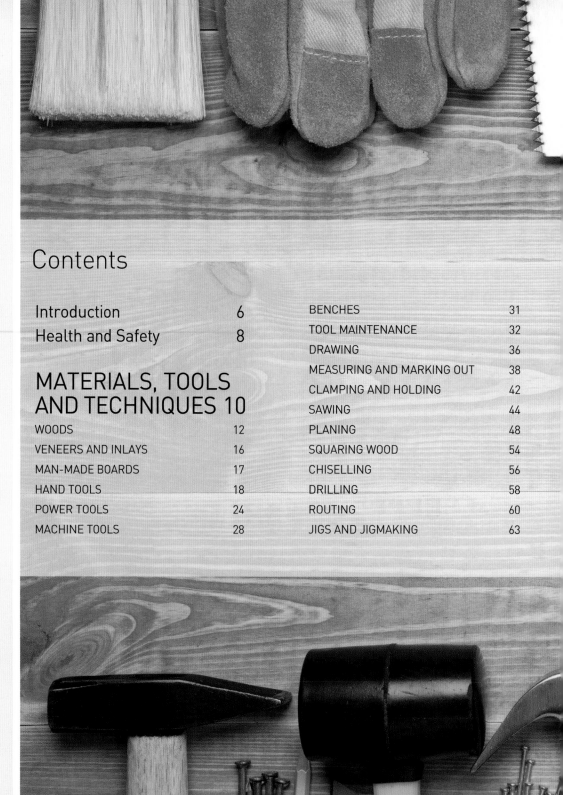

Contents

▲ SCOTT WOYKA
BURR OAK COFFEE TABLE

The oak tabletop is made from a huge tree, 2.4m (8ft) across, that remarkably turned out to be solid burr when processed into planks. The use of subtle curves for the top and understructure leaves the wood to speak for itself. Ash and cherry are also used. Techniques include coopering, shaping and through wedged tenons.

THE ENCYCLOPEDIA OF
Woodworking
TECHNIQUES

ROTATION STOCK

KT 2338104 3

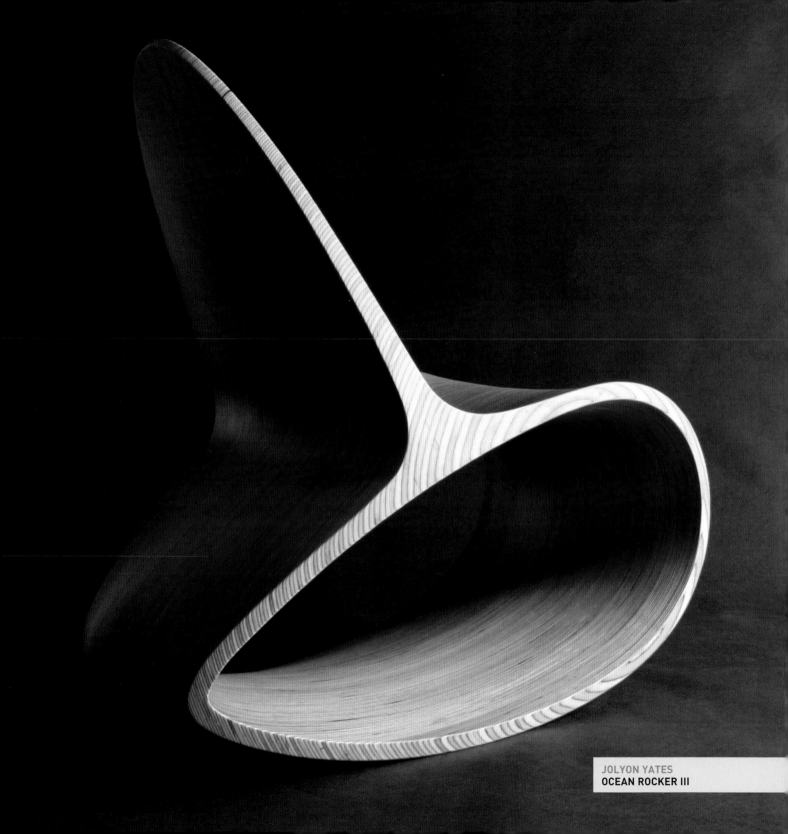

JOLYON YATES
OCEAN ROCKER III

Introduction

Wood never ceases to fascinate and engage us. It is our oldest natural resource, and the diverse ways in which it has been fashioned over the centuries tell the story of civilisation better than any other material. From tribal masks to wheels, pit props to paper for books, wood is unique.

As a material wood has remarkable character – it bends, it twists, it splits, it swells, it shrinks, it is fragrant, it can be almost transparent. It can be hard, soft, rigid or springy. It can last for centuries, or it can perish in seconds in fire.

There is hardly anything that has not been made of wood, and there is hardly anyone who is not drawn to its tactile and visual qualities. The infinite variety in the grain of wood has universal appeal, and it has enormous versatility both as a structural and decorative medium. It is one of the most popular materials to be fashioned today by both amateurs and professionals alike.

The traditions and techniques associated with woodworking have survived for centuries, and I believe that a mastery of technique underpins successful woodworking. I was fortunate enough to receive a firm grounding in hand-working techniques, and this fired my passion for designing in wood. The power tool revolution has not negated the old methods, but simply modified our approach. All tools, both hand and power operated, are a joy to work with, provided they are handled with skill. I hope this book goes some way towards explaining how this can be achieved.

Wood is a wonderful and satisfying material to use. Whenever you use it you will learn something new. Do not be put off by your lack of knowledge or experience, and do not be deterred by a fear of failure. Failure is an essential step to subsequent success. No number of words or photographs can tell you or show you what it is that makes the perfect joint – that you will find out for yourself as you work with different woods in different pieces, and, when you have acquired the 'knack', your confidence will grow and your command of technique will increase, enabling you to experiment still further with new designs.

Health and Safety

No subject has come to public attention in recent years more than health and safety. The popularity of woodworking and the consequent increase in the numbers of people involved in the activity have inevitably led to more accidents. Although legislation has been introduced to cover industrial and educational establishments, home woodworkers, who are usually working alone, are left to exercise their own discretion.

Health and safety should primarily be a matter of common sense, and no amount of legislation or safety guards on machines can prevent someone from cutting off a finger on a saw or severing a nerve by allowing a chisel to slip. Manufacturers invariably provide clear, comprehensive instructions for the safe operation of the tools and equipment they produce, and these should always be read carefully before any item is used.

However, health and safety also includes taking precautions against the dangers that can arise through dust and debris, and through noise pollution. Eye and ear protectors are essential and should always be worn. In addition, not only should you wear a respirator, but you should also use equipment that extracts dust at source. Noise pollution can be minimised by insulating individual pieces of equipment and, of course, the workshop itself.

Perhaps the greatest risk in the home workshop is from fire. Always sweep up dust and chippings at the end of the day and dispose of them carefully.

All-in-one respirator
This lightweight faceshield offers FFP2 protection against wood dust and most airborne particulate pollutants for around 8 hours using a tiny integral fan powered by a battery on the back of the cap. The filters are replaceable. The adjustable canvas cap makes room for the addition of a pair of ear muffs to complete the protection.

Half mask
A mask such as this is ideal especially for woodworkers who wear spectacles. The large non-return valve for low breathing resistance has a downward-facing exhalation valve to prevent the fogging of glasses or safety specs. The mask uses replaceable FFP3 filters to protect against airborne particles, oil aerosols, mists and fumes to 0.3 microns and above.

CHECKLIST
Power tools
- Always follow the manufacturer's instructions.
- When working with machinery, never wear loose clothing and always tie back long hair.
- Keep hands well away from moving or cutting edges.
- Wear ear protectors and goggles, especially when working a spindle moulder or power planer.
- Beware of trailing cables when using hand-held machinery.
- Always switch off at the mains before adjusting machinery.
- If in doubt, read or get some tuition before using any unfamiliar tools.
- Be sure all power tools and machines are correctly wired and insulated before use.

Workshop environment
- Keep the workshop well ventilated at all times.
- Always use a dustmask or visor in a dusty atmosphere.
- Be tidy; this saves time and prevents accidents.
- Always store flammable chemicals, lacquers, varnish etc, in a cool, safe place, ideally in a metal cabinet.

Using chemicals
- Avoid all skin contact with chemicals and glues.
- Wear gloves and goggles when using or mixing chemicals.

Earmuffs
You should wear earplugs or earmuffs to protect your hearing from long-term damage whenever you use power tools such as saws and routers. These soft, padded protectors are inexpensive, and it should soon become a matter of habit to put them on. Lightweight in-ear protectors are also available.

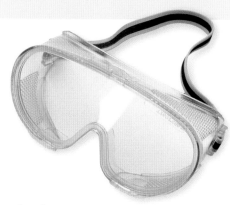

Goggles
Putting on a pair of goggles or a visor before you start work should become second nature. Eye injuries are the most commonly reported among woodworkers, and you should always wear some form of protection.

Dustmask
It is always worth buying the best possible quality dustmask. The well-known brands are usually best. Some brands are less effective than others, especially if they do not fit snugly around the contour of your nose. Some have nose clips. Make sure that they are rated FFP1 for light use and FFP2/3 for more demanding environments.

Materials, Tools and Techniques

Most wooden constructions integrate several techniques. When you are making a table, for example, the wood has to be selected and squared, and then the joints are marked out, sawn, chiselled and planed. The piece has to be glued and clamped, and finally finished. Not only are hand and power tools often used together but digital woodworking, such as CNC (computer numerical control) and laser cutting, is increasingly used today.

This section begins with an overview of materials and tools, and then uses step-by-step demonstrations to explain the basic techniques of woodworking, with hand- and power-tool options offered for each technique. Cross-references in the text will allow you to build up your knowledge quickly and, thus, your confidence. Each technique includes a checklist of essential equipment and a choice of items for hand- or power-tool enthusiasts.

◄ TOM VAUGHAN
S CHAIR
Made of European oak and finished with a natural hard wax oil, this chair is a physical 3D representation of the letter S, inspired by calligraphy and graffiti style. Designed by Tom Vaughan of the design and fabrication co-operative Object Studio, the chair pushed the makers to develop new methods of jointing timber, making this not only an aesthetic form but also a structurally sound and functional piece.

Woods

Of the many thousands of woods known to be in existence only a very small proportion is available commercially; of these no more than about 70 species could be said to be easily come by. Nevertheless there is still a large choice available and very often there are several species that may be equally suitable for the job in hand. The woods shown here are a small but representative selection of those in fairly common use.

Supplies of particular species are often very local, and most of us have to be content with what is available in the local supplier's yard or be prepared to wait, often a long time, for timber specially ordered.

Buying timber

There are many ways in which timber can be bought, all of which in some way affects its price. The cheapest method is to buy 'in the log', straight from the forest or timber yard as a tree trunk. If you have the means to convert it this is fine, but there are disadvantages, the most obvious being the uncertainty of the quality of the heartwood at the centre of the log, which might have a disappointing grain or colour.

Buying sawn boards is safer because the quality can be easily seen as the timber lies 'in stick' – that is, stacked one board above the other with small battens in between to allow air flow for drying.

The next step is to get your local mill to convert it to the sizes you want; this is known as buying 'rough-sawn'. Many timber merchants stock rough-sawn timber in a range of standard sizes and this is the bulk of the trade.

For the woodworker without a well-equipped workshop the easiest way is to buy 'prepared' timber; this is 'planed all round' on all four faces, and can very often be bought cut to length. Having passed through so many processes, this method of buying is the most expensive.

What to look for

What to look for depends on what you want. You may want a good figure on oak, for example, or be looking for heavy contrasts in the colour of yew. Sometimes it may be necessary to purchase a whole board in order to get the small section that you want.

Generally speaking, good straight-grained, clean wood free from knots is desirable but look for signs of warping. Heavy 'shakes' (splits) in a large oak beam may be acceptable but in a piece of pine for cabinetwork they are most unwelcome.

Types of timber

There are three ways in which timber is classified: trade name, local name or botanical name. The last of these is the only really safe one for identification. The main reason to know what you are buying is to ensure that the timber is suitable for its purpose. There are many hardwoods now on the market that were not exploited years ago and were introduced into the trade as substitutes for teak or mahogany and sold off as the real thing. Often they have similar properties but it is worth checking, especially if you are buying in quantity.

Hardwoods and softwoods

Hardwood refers to wood that comes from deciduous trees; softwoods come from coniferous trees. However, this terminology is something of a misnomer. Although hardwoods are generally hard and vice versa, there are exceptions. For example, yew is a softwood but it is extremely hard and can be difficult to work. Balsa is a hardwood and is very soft and can be cut and worked easily.

Storage before use

For the cabinet maker, movement in wood can be a great problem, especially in the modern centrally heated home. It is often difficult to know the moisture content of timber when it is first purchased, and without care, a beautifully crafted piece of furniture may shrink and open up after a few months in a heated atmosphere. You should always try to store your wood for some weeks in the environment in which the finished piece of furniture is going to be kept before starting work; if possible keep it in the actual house. This is not always possible but care in storage does pay dividends.

CEDAR OF LEBANON *softwood*
Characteristics A fine-textured resinous and sweet-smelling wood, usually fairly straight grained; poor bending qualities and low resistance to shock.
Uses Exterior work, greenhouses, garden furniture, light joinery.

PINE *softwood*
Characteristics Pale creamy yellow, usually straight grained and often knotty; generally fine or medium textured; works and glues well; low resistance to shock.
Uses Very commonly used in joinery, doors, window frames, etc; good source of turpentine and pitch.

ENGLISH YEW *softwood*
Characteristics Heavy lustrous wood with rich contrasts in colour from pale cream to brown and purple; bends well and finishes well; close, even grain.

Uses Longbows, small turnings such as lace bobbins and bowls, marquetry inlays, veneers.

EUROPEAN LARCH *softwood*
Characteristics Straight-grained, pale reddish brown heartwood, resinous and sometimes knotty; uniform texture; a tough timber that bends well and will take impact.
Uses Telegraph poles, boat planking, general joinery, pit props, veneers.

SCOTS PINE *softwood*
Characteristics Pale reddish brown, resinous and with clearly defined annular rings; troublesome in gluing due to high resin content; works well; low resistance to shock.
Uses Building construction, piles, pit props, joinery etc, veneers.

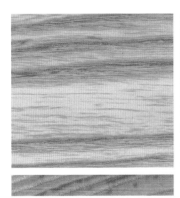

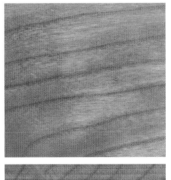

AMERICAN WHITE ASH
hardwood
Characteristics Greyish brown occasionally with a red cast; fairly coarse texture but generally even; bends well; stiff and strong with a good resistance to shock.
Uses A much used timber for handles such as in sports equipment, axes, garden tools, car bodies, joinery.

EUROPEAN BEECH *hardwood*
Characteristics Pinkish brown and very pale, will turn darker with steaming, occasionally with dark veins; texture fine, even and straight; bends exceptionally well and will glue easily; drill for nailing.
Uses Cabinet making, high-class joinery, tool handles, turnery.

AMERICAN CHERRY *hardwood*
Characteristics Fine, close and straight-grained wood, reddish brown and often flecked; a medium-strength timber that bends well and glues well; polishes to a high finish.
Uses Cabinet making, boat interiors, turning, inlay.

AMERICAN RED ELM *hardwood*
Characteristics Heavily marked with dark red stripes, works and bends exceptionally well; high resistance to shock loads; texture can be coarse but usually acceptable; glues and nails easily.

Uses Vehicle bodies, boatbuilding, wheel hubs, turnery, veneers.

BRAZILIAN MAHOGANY *hardwood*
Characteristics Light reddish brown to beautiful rich red; coarse to medium grain can be interlocked, often straight; not really suitable for bending; easy to glue, nail, stain and polish.
Uses Cabinet making, panelling, high-class furniture, boats, veneers.

FIGURED MYRTLE *hardwood*
Characteristics Anything from warm brown to yellow, maybe with a green tinge; texture firm and smooth; grain straight or irregular. A heavy timber with hard-wearing qualities.
Uses Panelling, flooring, turnery, joinery, cabinet making, marquetry.

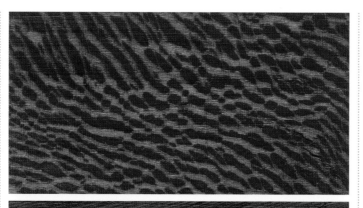

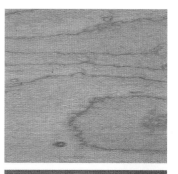

AMERICAN WHITE OAK *hardwood*
Characteristics Pale yellow to pink, normally straight grained with a figure on the quarter sawn; medium to coarse textured and light in weight; crushing strength medium, bends well.
Uses Joinery, cabinet making, flooring, ladders, coffins, cooperage, panelling, veneers.

LONDON PLANE/LACEWOOD *hardwood*
Characteristics Reddish brown, fairly light, very marked decorative rays on quarter sawn; medium texture, straight grain, sometimes fine; bends well and has medium strength.
Uses Turnery, cabinet making, joinery; highly prized for inlays and veneers; useful for panelling and light carcases.

AMERICAN MAPLE *hardwood*
Characteristics Creamy white to soft brown, straight grained, occasionally with flecks; bends reasonably well; medium strength in both bending and resistance to shock; nails, stains and polishes well.
Uses Cabinet making, joinery, flooring, turnery, panelling.

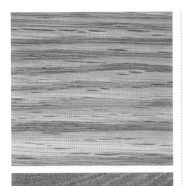

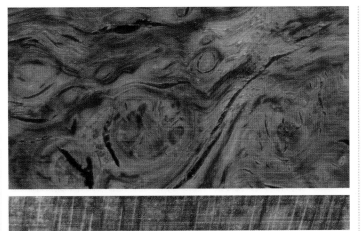

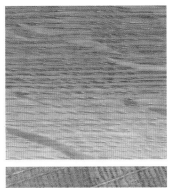

AMERICAN RED OAK *hardwood*
Characteristics Pinkish colour, possibly reddish; coarse, straight grain, not highly figured; medium bending strength but bends well; crushing strength high.
Uses Interior joinery, furniture, flooring, plywood, veneers.

BURR OAK *hardwood*
Characteristics Like all burrs, highly figured and visually exciting, virtually useless as structural timber but prized by turners and marquetarians; spotted and warty in appearance.

Uses Turnery, marquetry, inlay and general decorative purposes.

ENGLISH OAK *hardwood*
Characteristics Biscuit coloured or light brown; grain unpredictable, often straight, can be heavily interlocked; quarter sawn has distinctive rays; bends well but liable to stain if in contact with ferrous metals.
Uses Cooperage, boats, furniture, flooring, veneers.

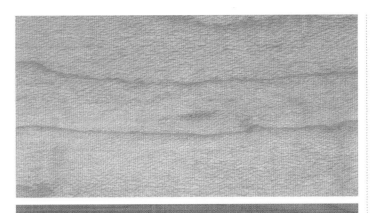

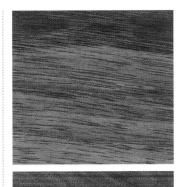

ROCK MAPLE *hardwood*
Characteristics White/creamy red, occasionally brown; variable grain from curly to straight; an even-textured wood with fine grain, bends well and retains high-strength characteristics; polishes, stains and glues reasonably well.
Uses Turnery, musical instruments, panelling, cabinet making, plywood.

AMERICAN BLACK WALNUT *hardwood*
Characteristics Dark brown to muddy purple, mainly straight grained but some curls; a dense, hard timber with a coarse grain, bends well; screws and nails well.
Uses Interior joinery, quality furniture, carving, turnery, veneers.

FRENCH WALNUT *hardwood*
Characteristics Brownish grey, sometimes darker, often streaky; irregular grain with a medium to coarse texture; bends reasonably well, average resistance to shock; takes a high finish.
Uses A first-rate cabinet timber, also for gunstocks, doors, carving, turnery, panelling, marquetry.

Veneers and Inlays

Fine cabinetwork, box making and musical instruments have for hundreds of years been enhanced by veneers and inlays. These are their main applications and, when well done, veneering is a technique that has been the benchmark of real quality. It also gives woodworkers nowadays a chance to use rare timbers otherwise out of reach.

Types of veneer
Left to right: aspen, Brazilian rosewood, olive ash, tropical olive, pomelle, pine, zebrano, cherry.

A range of bandings
These long patterned strips can be used with veneers or they can be placed in shallow grooves in solid timber, either as a decorative border or in a geometric or other patterned form.

A selection of marquetry motifs
These paper-backed, ready-made motifs are for use in marquetry projects.

Engineered veneers

Engineered veneers are manufactured from real wood (usually poplar). The wood is rotary peeled and processed into thin sheets, dyed throughout their thickness, then stacked, glued, and pressed or shaped. The new 'logs' are then squared up and sliced to produce veneers with consistent colour and grain.

Man-made Boards

Much of the ordinary domestic furniture bought today is manufactured from man-made boards such as plywood, chipboard and MDF. There are several reasons for this. Firstly it is cheap, secondly it is often veneered with highly expensive timbers that in the solid are not available, and thirdly because man-made boards come in large widths, they are very stable and will give no trouble in a warm, dry, centrally heated environment.

Man-made boards can also be environmentally friendly, in that they are often comprised of waste products from the mills, such as sawdust, bark and offcuts.

They are usually bonded with a resin that ties the particles together but has a devastating effect on tools unless they are tungsten-carbide tipped.

The cheapest of man-made boards, so far as the woodworker is concerned, is chipboard and this is literally made from bonded wood chips. It is ideal for cladding, cheap carcases and for making formers and templates for more exacting work.

Plywood is ideal for kitchen cabinets, tabletops, boatbuilding (marine ply) as well as shuttering, general cladding applications, toymaking and moulds and formers.

For really good dimensional stability blockboard and MDF are probably the best. Both will take veneer well and MDF in particular is very easy to work with in the field of furniture making.

There are many types, grades and thicknesses of man-made boards and all have very useful applications in modern woodworking.

Types of man-made boards

Below from left to right: hardboard, three-ply board, high-density (three-layer) chipboard, multi-layer ply, blockboard, birch multi-ply. Availability in large sizes is probably the greatest single selling point man-made boards have. This, coupled with world-wide availability, has made them indispensable.

MDF

MDF is useful in furniture making and notable for its ability to work well and hold a fine edge.

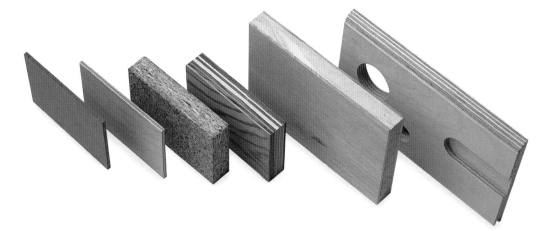

Hand Tools

Most woodworking tools are hand held – indeed, woodworking is itself a manual activity. However, tools that are operated by the muscles rather than an external power source are defined as 'hand tools'. When time is pressing, you may prefer to use a powered tool, but there are occasions when it is both quicker and more efficient to use a hand tool – when machines have to be set up, for instance – and hand tools are vital in measuring and marking out (see page 38), for no power tool – apart from a robot – can perform these tasks.

Some woodworkers prefer to use hand tools and to 'feel' the wood they are using with their fingers.

Hand tools are, in any case, an essential part of the kit of all woodworkers, and one of the great pleasures in woodworking is building up a collection of personal tools.

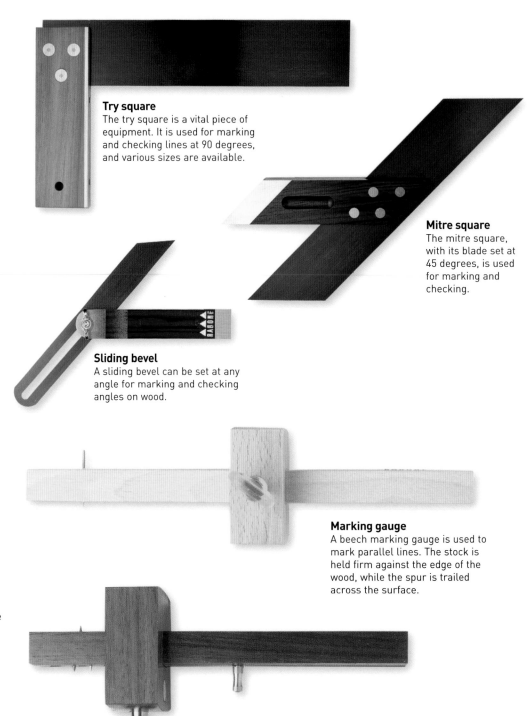

Try square
The try square is a vital piece of equipment. It is used for marking and checking lines at 90 degrees, and various sizes are available.

Mitre square
The mitre square, with its blade set at 45 degrees, is used for marking and checking.

Sliding bevel
A sliding bevel can be set at any angle for marking and checking angles on wood.

Marking gauge
A beech marking gauge is used to mark parallel lines. The stock is held firm against the edge of the wood, while the spur is trailed across the surface.

Mortise gauge
A mortise gauge, or combined mortise and marking gauge as it is sometimes known, has a single spur and two movable spurs, which can be set to the width of a mortise chisel. The stock is then held in position with its locking screw.

Japanese saw
The Kataba crosscut saw is typical of an increasingly popular range of Japanese hand tools. The saw cuts faster, has teeth facing backwards so is pulled (like a coping saw) and the blades are interchangeable.

Coping saw
A coping saw is essential for cutting fine, straight or curved lines, especially for removing waste from dovetails where a tenon saw is too large.

Dovetail saw
A dovetail saw is a miniature tenon saw for finer work. They are about 200mm (8in) long and have 16–22 teeth per 25mm (1in).

Tenon saw
A tenon saw is the best general-purpose saw for cutting straight lines. They are usually 300mm (12in) long and have 13–15 teeth per 25mm (1in).

Handsaw
Handsaws are either rip, crosscut or general purpose for cutting straight lines down or across the grain. They are approximately 650mm (25in) long and have 6–8 teeth per 25mm (1in).

Steel rule
The steel rule is not only accurate but is the strongest calibrated tool.

Marking knife
A marking knife, the most accurate scoring tool, is generally used against a straight-edge.

Bevel-edged chisel
Bevel-edged chisels, available in sizes from 3mm (⅛in) to 38mm (1½in), are lightweight, versatile tools. They can be used with a mallet but ideally not a hammer.

Firmer chisel
Available in the same size range, firmer chisels are more robust than bevel-edged chisels.

Mortise chisel
Cutting deep slots or mortises requires a stout tool, and mortise chisels range in size from 6mm (¼in) to 12mm (½in).

Rasp
Rasps and files are used for abrading. Coarser rasps remove stock quickly.

Spokeshave
For accurate shaping there is little to beat the spokeshave, which can have a flat or a rounded sole.

Smoothing plane
About 230mm (9in) long, the steel smoothing plane, with its fine blade adjustments, is a vital tool for flat and shaped skimming.

Block plane
The smaller block plane, which has a shallower blade angle, is used for delicate work.

Jack plane
The jack plane, which can be 350–387mm (13¾–15¼in) long, makes long pieces truer, and the extra weight gives more control.

Sharpening stones

The combination oilstone (far left) has coarse/medium or medium/fine grade surfaces. It is lubricated with oil and used to sharpen chisels and plane blades. The diamond stone (near left) has a grid of durable diamond particles set in plastic and uses water for lubrication.

Mallet

Claw hammer

Pin hammer

Striking tools

Striking tools are needed for a variety of purposes. Mallets, for example, are used to help drive chisels into wood (Mortise and Tenon Joints, **page 90**), while hammers are used to drive joints together or to nail joints. Mallets are usually made of beech, a very tough wood, and the striking action is slightly springier than with a hammer, which is used for sharper blows. Different types of hammer are available to suit light or heavy tasks.

Nail punch

Screwdrivers
There is always a place for a hand screwdriver even though screws are mostly power driven today. The main types are flat-headed, Phillips and Pozidrive, the latter two being suitable for power tool screwdriving as the bit locates the 'X'-indented screwhead easily.

Sash cramps
Sash cramps, which are available in 'bar' or 'pipe' section, range from 457mm (18in) to 1.2m (4ft).

'G' clamps
Whenever you need an extra pair of hands to hold your work, you will need a range of 'G' clamps. These vary from 25mm (1in) to 300mm (12in), and are remarkably versatile.

Power Tools

In recent decades the development of power tools has changed the face of woodworking significantly. Not only do these tools remove the drudgery from such arduous tasks as drilling and planing, but the ever-improving technology also offers new ways in which wood can be fashioned – the portable router with its huge array of routing bits is a good example. The development of tungsten-carbide tipped (TCT) blades, aluminium castings, plastics moulding (including softgrip plastics) and silicon chip technology has brought the power tool a long way from the simple portable drill or drill attachment. Smaller rare-earth motors and lithium-ion batteries are making possible more compact and powerful tools, adding to the versatility and convenience.

Cordless drill and bits

Available in voltages from 3.6 to 24, the cordless drill with keyless chuck can never be as powerful as its mains-operated counterpart, but it is safer and more convenient.

Drill bits

Twist drill bits, which range from 0.4mm (1/64in) to 12mm (1/2in) and which can have centre points, are used for general work.

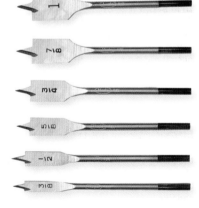

Flat bits

Flat bits (spade bits) make it possible to cut larger holes but using a narrow (6mm/1/4in) shank. They are available from 6mm to 38mm (1/4–1 1/2in).

Portable electric drill

The portable electric drill is the original power tool, and there can be few home workshops without one. With a keyed or fast-action chuck, a mains-powered drill typically operates on 550 watts with a 13mm (1/2in) chuck.

Jigsaw and blades

The jigsaw is a versatile handheld tool for making straight, curved or angled cuts. The blade moves up and down, and the cut is more efficient when the action is 'orbital'. Different blades are available for use with different materials.

Drill stand with drill

A vertical drill stand will accommodate a portable drill with a 43mm (1¾in) collar and permit more accurate drilling.

Electric plunging router

The most versatile tool in the workshop is the plunging router, which is basically an electric motor with a sharp rotating cutter at the end. With a huge variety of bits (cutters) and jigs (a straight fence is shown) available, the router can cut grooves, profile edges, cut joints and shape wood. They are available from 400 to around 2000 watts.

Router cutters

Router cutters are either high-speed steel (HSS) or the longer lasting tungsten-carbide tipped (TCT). Shank diameters are 6.38mm (¼in), 9mm (⅜in) or 12mm (½in).

Biscuit jointer

The biscuit jointer offers a versatile method of connecting solid board or sheet wood. The blade of a small circular saw is plunged to form elliptical recesses into which compressed wood 'biscuits' are glued.

Domino jointer

The domino jointer works on the same principle as a biscuit jointer, but uses a cutter to create a slot (mortise) into which a wooden 'domino' (tenon) can be inserted.

Portable circular saw

The portable circular saw is used to cut solid wood or manufactured board material. A straight fence can be attached for parallel cuts. The blade can be set to different depths for grooving, and the sole plate tilted for angled cuts along and across the grain. Blades are 125–230mm (5–9in) in diameter.

Disc and belt sander

This useful bench-mounted compact machine uses the same electric motor to power a disc sander and finisher. The latter has a continuous sanding belt.

Portable vacuum press

Portable vacuum presses for applying veneers give the home woodworker an easy-to-achieve professional result. The glued elements are placed inside the vacuum bag; a vacuum pump then removes the air so that the veneer bonds to the substrate material.

Random orbit sander

The random orbit sander has a self-gripping backed abrasive disc that moves eccentrically while it rotates to create a random abrading effect. It is used for flat and curved work.

Orbital sander

The orbital sander uses ½ or ⅓ size abrasive sheets, which are clamped to a padded baseplate. The action is elliptical, and the tool should be used under its own weight.

Machine Tools

Not many years ago, a powered planer or circular saw would have weighed tons and would have taken up so much space in a workshop that there would have been no room for anything else. Today the availability of small powered machine tools has made precise and imaginative work possible for both amateurs and professionals.

Cast aluminium has replaced heavy steel in the manufacture of the components, and the efficiency of the motors has increased as their size has diminished. Some, such as the mini planer-thicknessers, have become so small that they are as portable as power tools. Others, such as the spindle moulder, can perform the same tasks and have the same capacity as some of the largest electric routers.

The variety and portability of the modern, lightweight machine tools makes planning and setting up a workshop much easier. When you are siting these tools, you must leave space for the 'infeed' and 'outfeed' of the wood, but, if space is limited, remember that not all these tools have to be bolted to the floor, and they can be moved into position when they are needed.

All woodworking tools, especially powered items, are potentially dangerous. Strict safety procedures should always be followed, including the positioning of safety guards, whenever they are used.

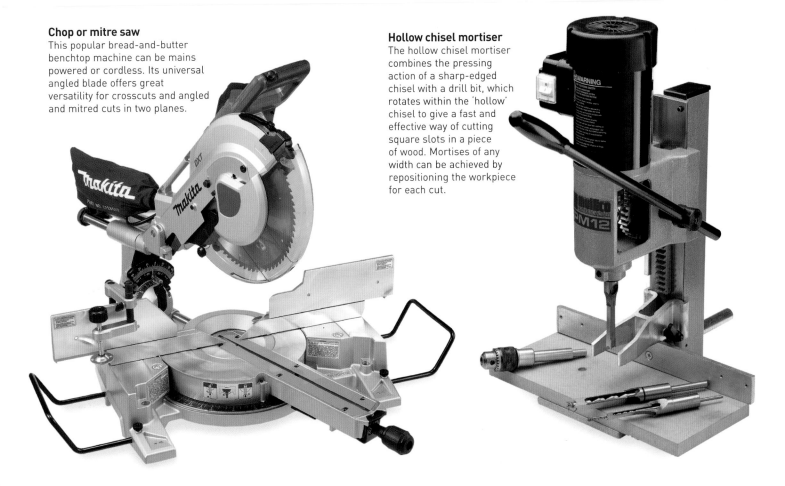

Chop or mitre saw
This popular bread-and-butter benchtop machine can be mains powered or cordless. Its universal angled blade offers great versatility for crosscuts and angled and mitred cuts in two planes.

Hollow chisel mortiser
The hollow chisel mortiser combines the pressing action of a sharp-edged chisel with a drill bit, which rotates within the 'hollow' chisel to give a fast and effective way of cutting square slots in a piece of wood. Mortises of any width can be achieved by repositioning the workpiece for each cut.

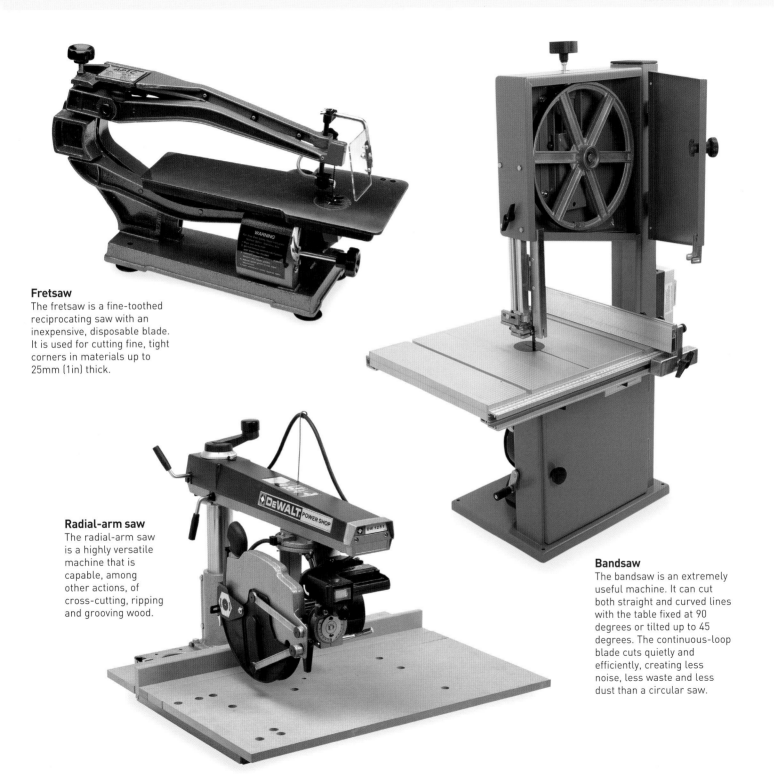

Fretsaw
The fretsaw is a fine-toothed reciprocating saw with an inexpensive, disposable blade. It is used for cutting fine, tight corners in materials up to 25mm (1in) thick.

Radial-arm saw
The radial-arm saw is a highly versatile machine that is capable, among other actions, of cross-cutting, ripping and grooving wood.

Bandsaw
The bandsaw is an extremely useful machine. It can cut both straight and curved lines with the table fixed at 90 degrees or tilted up to 45 degrees. The continuous-loop blade cuts quietly and efficiently, creating less noise, less waste and less dust than a circular saw.

Planer-thicknesser

The planer-thicknesser, as its name suggests, combines the actions of planer and thicknesser. It can be used to plane the wood to create a flat surface and then, using the fence, to square the edges. As a thicknesser it enables the wood to be machined parallel to the already dressed surfaces by means of an automatic feed. In some models, the surfacing table swings clear when the thicknesser action is in use.

Bench grinder

This is used for repairing the edges of chisels and plane blades before they are honed (sharpened). The whetstone grinder shown here has a tray for water to lubricate the grinding action. Added is a jig to set the correct blade angle when grinding. Non-ferrous metals should not used on grinders, because they will clog the wheels.

Woodturning lathe

The woodturning lathe is one of the simplest machine tools, and it has the additional advantage that complete objects can be made on it. The wood is pre-cut into a more or less circular shape, mounted on to the lathe – either on a faceplate or between centres – and spun at speed. A gouge or scraper against a toolpost is fed against the revolving wood.

Benches

The woodworker's bench is the centre of the workshop, from where all creativity springs. A bench should be sturdy and level, and at a height that suits you. It offers a flat, supporting surface, but should also include a vice and 'dogs' to hold work. The best benches are made of seasoned beech, but you can improvise and build your own from reclaimed timber. Above all, a bench should withstand the wrenching or shuddering caused by vigorous planing (see page 48) in the vice, when you put your entire weight behind the plane. Apart from the traditional bench, there are numerous ingenious folding and lightweight devices that grip wood in a variety of ways.

Portable folding bench or 'Workmate'

This folding bench is a superbly designed device. It takes up little room when it is not needed, but can grip or support awkwardly shaped work in its double vice jaw top and plastic 'dogs'. Extra support can be achieved when planing if you place one foot on the 'step'. The bench's versatility extends to gripping circular sections of wood of large and small diameters. However, its lightweight construction means that it is not designed to take a pounding from a mallet.

The workbench

The classic European workbench. This model has a slot along the back edge in which to store tools, and a shelf beneath the top to hold pieces of wood and large items of equipment. The sturdy worktop is made of beech (in North America benchtops are traditionally in maple). The continental-style wooden vices grip firmly without marking the wood.

Tool Maintenance

All woodworking tools need maintaining, even if it is only a light coating of oil to prevent a steel blade from rusting. Many woodworking tools have a sharp cutting edge and, apart from files and 'hard-tipped' saws (which are discarded when blunt), these edges need truing up, setting, honing – or in some cases – grinding, to restore them to optimum working order.

The importance of a razor-sharp edge for a marking knife, a plane blade or chisel can only be emphasised by describing the effects of using blunt tools.

Blunt tools are virtually useless and lead to disastrous results: a blunt marking knife tears rather than incises the grain, a blunt chisel fails to cut. The beginner may also not realise that the cutting angle of the chisel greatly affects its performance irrespective of the keenness of its tip.

The importance of regular maintenance

Increasingly, hand- and powered saws have hard-tipped blades that offer many times the life of re-sharpenable blades but are thrown away when dulled. It is not always apparent when the cutting edge is dull. Only comparison with a replacement blade/tool makes it obvious.

To get the most out of your tools, you should maintain them regularly. A chisel blade dulls every time it is worked into the grain. It takes seconds to 'touch up' or hone the blade on an oilstone. Many new tools are supplied either blunt or crudely sharpened, so the ritual of grinding and honing should begin as soon as the tool is taken from its box.

Router cutters (see Routing, page 60) need proper care and servicing as they are expensive, brittle and prone to resin clogging, which leads to heat build-up and fast blunting because of the high speed of revolution. Woodworking is about care, attention and pride and this starts with your own tools.

CHECKLIST
- **Oilstone**
- **Slipstone**
- **Light oil**
- **Diamond stone**
- **Burnishing tool**
- **Flat file**
- **Triangular small file**
- **Bench, vice and saw battens**
- **Health and safety (pages 8–9)**

Dismantling and grinding a plane blade

The modern steel smoothing or jack plane is a precision instrument and requires proper setting up each time the blade is taken out for sharpening. This should be done frequently as a plane can never be sharp enough and dulls each time it engages with the wood. Even if a handplane is suddenly jolted or dropped against the benchtop, the blade can be knocked out of true. A handplane needs constant attention, adjusting and – above all – keeping razor sharp. To dismantle the plane, lift the lever on the lever cap and lift out the blade assembly.

1 The cap can be used as a screwdriver for tightening the blade-assembly screw for the correct cap lever pressure. Use the cap to unscrew the cap-iron screw and then take the blade apart ready for grinding or sharpening.

BLADE ANGLES

Chisels are bought from the manufacturer already ground at an angle of 25 degrees, and then they are honed further to an angle of 30 to 35 degrees, using an oilstone.

Simply place the chisel's bevelled edge on the stone, raise the chisel handle very slightly to obtain the additional angle and work the chisel back and forth until a fine new bevel is formed. Follow the same procedure for a plane blade.

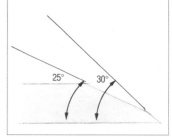

5 Now the plane blade is 'backed off' to remove the burr that the sharpening has caused. Repeat the sharpening and backing off process. Finally the fine burr is removed with a leather strop or by simply cutting into the edge of a piece of wood.

2 Normally the plane blade requires only occasional grinding, if a nick has been taken off the edge. Here the electric bench grinder is used. Feed the blade against the wheel at an angle of about 35 degrees. Move the blade sideways across the wheel using the fingers to maintain pressure at a fixed angle.

3 It takes some practice to grind a blade neatly. The important thing to do is maintain a consistent angle. To help, you can mark the blade where the toolrest makes contact. Never grind bevels or curves on the plane blade. The blade should be perfectly straight across.

4 It is important to sharpen just one side of the blade (the ground-angled side) and to leave the other side absolutely flat. Hold the plane blade firmly with both hands. The motion and the spread of the fingers and locking of the wrists helps maintain the angle (about 25 degrees). Work the blade into the oilstone or diamond stone in a series of definite forwards/ backwards strokes.

6 The cap iron is screwed back on to the plane blade, leaving a gap of about 2mm (1/12in) at the tip. This is crucial for forming the shaving, and perfect contact should exist between these two pieces of metal to avoid shavings becoming trapped in between them.

7 When you have inserted the blade assembly back into its housing, the final adjustments are made with the screw adjuster and tilting lever. Turn the plane upside down and look down the sole using screw and lever to adjust the blade, so it protrudes fractionally giving a parallel shadow.

Sharpening a chisel
1 Chisels need frequent sharpening just like plane blades. Grip the chisel with both hands and work the blade in the same way as for sharpening a plane blade. The locking of the wrists helps prevent a curved edge from forming.

2 Sharpening the chisel blade at a slightly shallower angle increases its cutting efficiency, though in theory it makes the tip more brittle.

Sharpening a scraper

1 Any oblong piece of quality steel can be used as a scraper. Its cutting action relies on a burr that is formed by first draw filing the edge flat. Use both hands on the file and work it up and down the scraper edge. The scraper is first mounted low in a vice.

2 Now use a slipstone or diamond stone to hone the edge of the blade. A burr is created by stroking the scraper with a burnisher a few times with the blade down against the benchtop. Now the burr is turned by stroking each edge of the blade at a slight angle with the burnisher.

Grinding and sharpening a marking knife

1 A cordless grinder can be extremely useful around the workshop for grinding tools such as the marking knife. Here both edges are fed into the wheel with the rotation against the blade so that the burr is removed.

2 The marking knife should be constantly sharpened on an oilstone, using a light oil for lubrication.

Care of planer blades

Planer blades are usually throwaway TCT or re-sharpenable high-grade steel. It is not advisable to re-grind planer blades. They should be sent away for servicing, but minimal honing can be done to extend their life. It should be remembered that planer blades are balanced and that means they are identical in profile.

1 To remove or reset the planer cutters, first use a spanner to release the cutters from the clamps.

2 It is essential that both cutters are set identically in their seatings and this can be checked with two battens with marks aligning the outfeed table and the tip of the cutters. The cutters should just 'kiss' the wood on both battens. Adjustments to raise the cutters can be made with the Allen key and spring-loaded grub screws.

Lubricating planer tables

Most home workshop or light-industrial planer-thicknessers have aluminium beds, which means they tend to stick occasionally. At times a lubricant such as baby talcum powder can be applied to the thicknessing table surface to facilitate the automatic feed of the wood.

Care of routers and cutters

1 Router cutters or bits are expensive and fragile. Apart from careful storage in a box, they require regular maintenance, not least of all removal of wood resin from the cutting edge. Carefully hone the inside edges of cutters on a sharpening stone; use a diamond stone for TCT cutters. Do not hone the outside edges as the precisely balanced cutting action will be disturbed.

2 This tool creates dust, and it is the dust that can be a menace to its proper efficiency. Use a light oil to lubricate the plunge mechanism.

Grinding flat bits

With care flat bits can be 'touched up' on the grinder but excessive grinding will upset the balance of the identical cutters.

Grinding gouges

Gouges for turnery and carving are easily ground by rotating them slowly at a fixed angle against the toolpost of the grinder. Use the fingers as a seating for the rotating action.

Care of saws

The following steps give an overview of the process of sharpening a saw, but this is a difficult tool for an amateur to sharpen. Nowadays, most woodworkers send their saws to a 'saw doctor' rather than try to do it themselves. In addition, many saws have hard-tipped blades that cannot be re-sharpened; they offer many times the life of traditional blades and are thrown away when dulled.

1 First mount the saw between two straight pieces of wood in a vice and use a file to 'top' the teeth level. Sometimes a file-holding jig is used but you can acquire the knack by holding the file in the forefinger and thumb of each hand and using the other fingers as a guide against the face of the saw to set up a firm filing motion.

2 The saw blade is now 'set' with a special tool that bends each alternate tooth to a specific angle (adjusted on the tool according to the points per inch).

3 The final stage is to use a triangular-section file to file each tooth so that it is sharp. Get into the motion of filing the alternate teeth and then repeat the action from the other side on the other teeth. A little candle wax applied to the saw blade helps with the action.

Drawing

Many woodworkers regard drawing as an unnecessary chore, and some even find it daunting. Indeed it is not vital to be able to draw when working with wood, other than to possess basic measuring and marking out skills (see page 38).

However, if you wish to become a versatile practitioner of this craft, an ability to draw and understand drawings is a great advantage. This is true whether you wish to design your own woodwork or merely copy plans. It would be a genius who could conceive of and execute a new piece of work without resorting to some kind of drawing or visualisation on paper, even if only on the back of an envelope.

CHECKLIST
- **Proprietary drawing board or A3 (11 x 17in) piece of melamine-faced 18mm (¾in) chipboard or something similar**
- **Tee square**
- **30 degree and 45 degree set squares**
- **60cm (24in) plastic ruler**
- **Protractor**
- **French curves**
- **Scaled ruler**
- **Pair of compasses**
- **Various grades of pencil**
- **Fibre-tips or drawing pens**
- **Masking tape or board clips**

Getting ideas down on paper
1 With a little practice, quick freehand perspective sketching comes easily. You may prefer to use a fibre-tip pen or a soft-leaded pencil, such as a 2B.

2 The hand naturally draws lines in a clean sweep (the wrist serves as a pivot point), so constantly turn the paper to draw each line with ease.

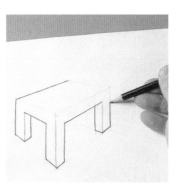

3 A series of light lines can build up the picture quickly. Then go over with a bolder line for the outline. Leading edges are usually thickened. (In most drawing there are three types of line: a feint projection line, the outline and the dimension line.)

Drawing circles
1 Perspective circles or curves can be drawn within a grid, which can be very helpful! Try drawing the circle first within a quartered box, then draw the same box at an angle and fill in the curves. Remember to rotate the paper and use your hand naturally.

After a while you will be able to draw perspective circles freehand. Remember that it is an ellipse that has its long arc perpendicular to the walls of the cylindrical object to be drawn.

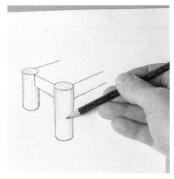

2 Circular solids can be shaded to give depth. Imagine a series of equidistant points marked around the circle and extend the lines vertically.

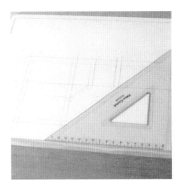

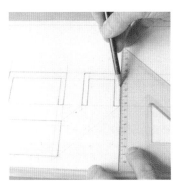

Translating sketches into working drawings

1 More accurate drawings can be achieved on a drawing board with tee square, set square and ruler. First set up the paper on the board using masking tape. You need H and 2H pencils. When working with a tee square, always ensure it is tight against the edge of the board.

2 Plans for woodworking usually consist of a front elevation, end elevation and a plan (bird's-eye view). There are two conventions: first-angle and third-angle projections. A horizontal and vertical axis are drawn first with a hard-leaded pencil.

3 Shared information such as the height of the object to be drawn, its width and other features can be extended or projected in feint lines to all three elevations. Transferring this information from the plan to the end elevation can be achieved with the 45 degree set square.

4 The outline then depicts each elevation boldly and, as a general rule, the projection line should not be seen beyond arm's length (provided you have used a 2H pencil). Hidden details can be shown on each elevation using a dotted-line convention.

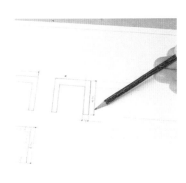

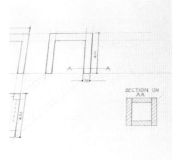

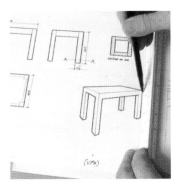

5 Dimension lines are then included in the drawing, spreading the information evenly across the three elevations.

You will probably need to make working drawings to scale, say one-fifth scale. Specially scaled rulers can be used for this.

6 To be useful, a working drawing requires the addition of detailed information that needs further clarification. Enlarged detailed elevations or sections can be drawn elsewhere on the paper, cross referring with a code such as 'Section AA'.

7 You may wish to trace the entire working drawing using a fibre-tip or drawing pen on a thin drawing sheet, implementing a perspective view of the object that has been separately drawn. This helps balance the layout of the drawing. Either tape the sheets down or use heavy (but clean) objects to anchor the paper while drawing.

8 A useful application of simple technical drawing in woodworking is the construction of a cutting list.

Measuring and Marking Out

It is very rare in woodworking to take the tools straight to the material without first marking the wood or setting everything out. Precision is crucial for accurate working. This may be acceptable for a tomato box – accurate perhaps to 3mm (⅛in) or so – but not for a piece of cabinetry for which accuracy may need to be as fine as half a millimetre (about ¹⁄₆₄in) or even less. Often mistakes made later on in the making of a piece can be attributed to poor measuring and marking out.

The simplest measuring is achieved with a measuring stick (any flat and straight piece of wood) and marks can be transferred from one piece of wood to another, such as the identical lengths of table legs. Indeed after the initial measurement has been taken with a calibrated rule, it is often more accurate to copy subsequent components from the original, which in effect becomes the 'measuring stick'.

Some woodworking joints are measured out on one piece first, cut with the saw and chisel, then copied on to the other piece (see Dovetail Joints, page 94), whereas other joints are marked independently for maximum accuracy (see Mortise and Tenon Joints, page 90).

Choice of marker

What is crucial to accurate marking out, whether you use a measuring stick, steel rule or other aids, is the choice of marker. Effective marking out is bold and precise, and the areas to be cut away as 'waste' are shaded clearly. Traditionally, woodworkers use a pencil or marking knife; increasingly, ballpoint pens are used. A pencil tends to blunt as it draws, which makes a wider and less accurate line (unless it is a hard pencil and then it can be difficult to see the mark). The marking knife gives the most accurate results but leaves an incised mark, difficult to remove afterwards and allowing no margin of error for beginners.

The most fundamental rule of all in measuring and marking is to check, check and check again.

CHECKLIST
- **Pencil, ballpoint pen, marking knife**
- **Try square**
- **Steel rule**
- **Tape measure**
- **Measuring stick(s)**
- **Marking gauge**
- **Combination square**
- **Mitre square**
- **Sliding bevel**
- **Mortise gauge**
- **Trammel**
- **Pair of compasses**
- **Centre square**
- **Health and safety (pages 8–9)**

Measuring and marking parallel lines
1 There are various ways to measure and mark parallel lines. The easiest is to use a tape measure, stepping off two marks at either end of the board. But you can also use a steel rule or measuring sticks.

2 A steel straight-edge or steel rule can be used to mark a line across the two measured points. Spread your fingers along the straight-edge to ensure it does not slip. Mark the line up to the edge of the rule.

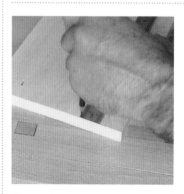

Measuring to length
1 When cutting boards to length (see Squaring Wood, page 54), it is always best to start off with a fresh 'squared' edge. Measure in with the rule about 6mm (¼in) to square the first line across. (This is the minimum distance for sawing without the fibres disintegrating, and when this happens control of the saw is very difficult.)

2 Set the zero at the 6mm (¼in) mark and measure off the required dimension, spreading the fingers again to keep the steel rule steady.

Squaring lines

1 A marking knife and try square are used to square the lines across. The marking knife is more accurate, although a pencil can be used.

2 When using a try square (which is fixed at exactly 90 degrees), always squeeze the stock against the edge of the wood, using all fingers. Carefully score a line with the knife tight against the steel blade of the square.

3 Extend the line all the way around the wood, using the try square against the face side and face edge with their respective reference marks.

Shading/duplicating lengths

Waste is traditionally shaded with a pencil and, when two or more pieces are to be cut, spacing lines are drawn for the saw thickness. Duplicate lengths are easily measured off by using a measuring device such as abrasive paper.

Marking out a row of dovetails

1 Here we show how dovetails can be accurately marked out; this technique can be applied to any panel where equal divisions are required. Equal divisions can be stepped off by using a tape measure diagonally. With both edges of the wood, line up the chosen graduations and step off the intervals. Use a try square against the end of the wood to extend these marks parallel to the sides to meet the end.

2 On the wood, mark a shoulder line that is the thickness of the other piece of wood. Then use a dovetail template and steel rule to mark the dovetail pitch. To do this, step off 3mm ($\frac{1}{8}$in) marks either side of each vertical line, align the template and mark each dovetail. Shade in the waste afterwards.

3 As a general rule, an extra 1mm (about $\frac{1}{32}$in) should be added to the distance of joint shoulder lines to allow for cleaning up afterwards. If the shoulder line is exactly the same thickness as the wood, then the thickness of that wood has to be planed undersize when cleaning the joint up.

Using other marking squares
1 A mitre square can be used like a try square but for fixed 45 degree angles. Here both tools are used to mark alternately all the way around the wood.

2 A combination square is a versatile tool with a sliding straight-edge. It can be used as a try square or mitre square.

3 The length of the straight-edge (which is also a rule) can be adjusted to suit the task.

4 Here the combination square is being used as a simple gauge for pencilling parallel lines.

Using a marking gauge
1 A marking gauge is used for marking parallel lines. Its adjustable stock is secured to the stem with a screw. A pointed spur makes the mark. A steel rule is used to measure the setting, then the gauge is used very firmly against the edge of the wood.

2 You can hold the wood in the vice or support it against a bench stop when using a marking gauge.

3 A quick way to set a marking gauge to the centre of a piece of wood is to first set the gauge by guessing, then step off a mark from each side. Finally intersect the marks with the spur and set. Fine adjustments can be made by banging the locked gauge against the benchtop to fractionally move the stock along the stem.

Using a mortise gauge
The practice of knocking a gauge for fine setting should not be used on a mortise gauge, which has a brass double spur adjuster. The two spurs are set to the width of a mortise chisel (see Mortise and Tenon Joints, page 90) and then the stock is set to the appropriate position by repeating the centring method.

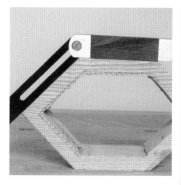

5 A sliding bevel can be adjusted to any angle for measuring work. Here again the stock should be held firmly against the edge of the wood.

6 The sliding bevel can mark or check both external and internal angles. It is tightened by a screw or wing nut.

Marking circles and radii

Mark circles and radii with a pair of compasses, first using them to step off the centre mark from adjacent edges.

Other marking operations

1 It is easy to make a trammel for scribing small and large curves. One end is drilled to take a ballpoint pen and a panel pin is used as a centre point at the required measured distance.

2 Finding the centre of circular pieces of wood such as turnery blanks (see Turning Wood, page 108) can be achieved with a workshop-made centre square. Two adjacent positions give a cross. Slightly irregular circles can be marked by stepping off a series of random marks around the circumference.

3 Measuring sticks are immensely useful in woodworking. Here two small offcuts are used to accurately measure internal lengths. The sticks are overlapped and a mark placed across them.

4 The importance of coding pieces of work not only helps minimise confusion when rearranging several identical pieces, but their exact positions can also be easily marked off ready for gluing and assembly (see Gluing, page 66).

Clamping and Holding

The need to hold work securely is important in woodworking. If the workpiece itself is not secured, you will not be able to operate tools efficiently and safely. For example, no matter how steady your hand is at sawing, if the wood is not held firmly the saw will jam in the cut. This leads to frustration, unsatisfactory results and possibly injury. There are also times when just one pair of hands is not enough and improvised holding devices are needed. As you progress in woodworking you will probably find that you can make your own, to suit your own needs.

CHECKLIST
- **Woodworking bench**
- **Bench-hook**
- **Woodworkers vice**
- **'G' or 'quick-release' clamps**
- **Sash cramps or long 'quick-release' clamps**
- **Hot-melt glue gun**
- **Bench stops**
- **Double-sided tape**
- **Health and safety (pages 8–9)**

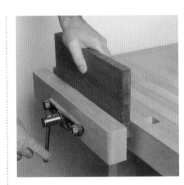

The woodworking bench
Apart from being a firm and solid base, the woodworking bench is the most basic holding and supporting device. Incorporated into it is usually a metal or wooden vice that supports work up to about 150mm (6in) wide. Metal vices should be faced with a stout hardwood. This is to avoid bruising the wood being held. Holes to secure the wooden faces are almost always pre-drilled by the manufacturers, and wooden faces are fitted by the user. As a general rule keep the workpiece as low as possible in the vice to avoid vibration or 'chatter' when sawing or planing.

Using a vice
1 The vice can hold work in a variety of ways, for instance, using the benchtop as extra support. For planing curves, short work can be gripped end-to-end. To plane you simply release the pressure and rotate the wood after each cut.

2 Awkward holding situations can be overcome by tilting the workpiece at an angle in the vice, giving steady support for planing or sawing.

Using 'G' and 'quick-release' clamps
1 A variety of 'G' or 'quick-release' clamps is essential workshop kit. Two clamps on the bench can firmly support the work for chiselling, sawing and drilling. Use scrapwood to prevent the clamp from damaging the workpiece.

2 Sash cramps or long 'quick-release' clamps are available in various lengths. They are suitable for holding work together during gluing (see page 66).

Using a bench-hook
A bench-hook (which can be easily made) is an excellent partner to the vice, and this will give you extra stability when sawing wood.

Using a sash cramp
To support long or extra wide work, the vice can accommodate a sash cramp with packing blocks. A sash cramp mounted in the vice is also particularly useful for planing long square work, to make it circular. This is done by planing away the sharp edges. Firstly from 4 to 8 (rotating as you go), then from 8 to 16 and so on, until the workpiece is round.

Using an end vice and dogs
If you support a thin workpiece in a vice, it may bow under the pressure; the benchtop is better because the workpiece can lie flat upon it. Some workbenches include an end vice that operates with insertable dogs. These are pieces of wood or plastic that are inserted into pre-cut holes along the bench's length. The holes are spaced about 150mm (6in) apart.

Using a bench stop
For planing thin wood a bench stop can be improvised by using a 'G' clamp to hold a thinner piece of plywood on to the benchtop. Make sure it is large enough for the planing action not to foul the clamps.

Using folding workbenches
1 Modern universal folding workbenches incorporate plastic dogs that can hold virtually any shaped work. These cleverly designed devices can be very useful, especially when used for planing or sawing.

2 They can support circular-sectioned work both horizontally and vertically.

The hot-melt glue gun
Use a hot-melt glue gun to temporarily hold a workpiece in position. Apply glue 'blobs' and allow to cool slightly on four points of the workpiece. Press the workpiece on to the workbench where it is ideal for routing operations when a vice or clamp might foul the router fence. The bond is only temporary and the workpiece can be prised off.

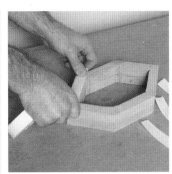

Using adhesive tape
Double-sided adhesive tape is remarkably strong for temporarily securing work to the bench, or for securing jig templates to the workpiece.

Sawing

The saw is one of the oldest tools and its action is very simple. A series of teeth are set outwards in alternate directions along a flat steel blade and sharpened to a critical angle. This angle is determined by the type of work the saw has to do. The saw cuts a channel in the wood by severing the fibres rather like a row of miniature chisels. The groove the saw cuts is fractionally wider than the thickness of the saw in order to give clearance. This is called the 'saw kerf'. Because wood behaves differently along the grain from the way it does across the grain, there are saws for ripping and for crosscutting. These are differentiated by their number of teeth and pitch angle. There is a family of finer toothed saws with thinner blades that are reinforced by a backing strip and these are called 'backsaws', of which the tenon saw is the most common.

The technique of sawing by hand has to be learned by practice, and it depends for its success very largely on the quality and correct setting of the tool. Most woodworkers nowadays have saws set and sharpened by 'saw doctors', but buying a quality saw in the first place will eliminate a lot of problems.

Saws for cutting curves include pad saws, coping saws and bow saws, although these have now been largely superseded by powered saws.

Power saws

The marriage of modern saw blade technology and electric power has resulted in extremely accurate and smooth cutting saws, relying on the harder wearing tungsten carbide (TC) for the tips. These 'tipped' saws are more expensive but easily prove their worth in their cutting abilities and duration of service.

The radial-arm saw is an overhead circular saw with a universally angled saw head. It uses a standard circular saw blade, or for wider cuts for jointing it uses multi-cutters called dado heads. A chop or mitre saw is a type of overhead circular saw that is useful for cutting pieces to length quickly and accurately, as well as cutting mitres. A track saw is essentially a circular saw that can clip onto and slide along a track laid on the workpiece, and is especially useful for cutting sheet material such as MDF.

Perhaps the most efficient, and quietest, of powered saws is the bandsaw with its narrow continuous blade running around either two or three wheels, one of which is electrically driven. The flexible blade makes it suitable for cutting curves and straight lines. It also has a deceptive capacity for cutting thick boards. The

convenient smaller versions of these electric saws are portable circular saws and jigsaws.

Dust extraction should be used, especially with circular-type saws where debris is thrown out centrifugally.

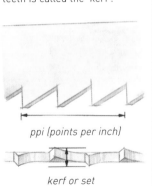

SAW SPECIFICATION

A saw blade is specified by points per inch (PPI) or teeth per inch (TPI). The 'set' of the teeth is called the 'kerf'.

ppi (points per inch)

kerf or set

Using a handsaw

The handsaw can be used for cutting wood of fairly thick dimensions either across or along the grain. When designed for cutting along the grain they are known as rip saws, and when for across the grain as crosscuts. They are however to some extent interchangeable. The rip saw has a wider 'set' on the teeth because working down the grain of the wood it has more difficulty in clearing away the waste. Crosscutting severs the fibres

cleanly and is therefore less of a problem. You can support the wood by clamping it to the bench or supporting it lower on a saw horse or any firm base.

First draw a line across the wood (the line can be extended down the edge). This makes the cut easier to 'sight up'. You can use the thumb of your supporting hand to guide the path of the saw initially. Draw the saw gently back to start the motion of the first cut, guiding the flat side of the blade against your upturned thumb.

Grip the handle firmly with the forefinger pointing forwards to give greater control over the stroke. You may need to use a knee to support the wood. Once the first and most difficult cut is made, use a steady motion to saw through the board. Jamming the saw in its groove can be avoided if you ensure your eye is directly in line with the saw blade, thus avoiding sideways pressure.

  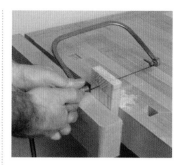 

Using a backsaw

1 The backsaw, such as a tenon or dovetail saw, produces a cleaner and more accurate cut than a handsaw. Secure the wood in a bench-hook and draw the saw gently back across the wood against the end of the hook on the waste side of the cutting line. Work the saw back along the wood to make a full-width saw channel, then switch to smooth back and forth strokes to complete the cut.

2 The backsaw can be used for cutting along and across the grain. Support the wood in the vice to free your other hand to use a two-handed grip for extra control.

The greatest difficulty in using a backsaw is in maintaining a 'square' cut and not wandering off the line. Always keep your eye directly above and in line with the blade, and closely monitor the first few cuts – stop, look and correct the path of the saw as necessary.

Using a coping saw

1 Whereas a tenon saw can only saw straight into the wood, the coping saw is useful for cutting curves or removing stock quickly. Hold the saw with both hands. Generally the teeth cut on the backward stroke but you will find it works both ways. The blade can be rotated and set by twisting the handle so that the saw cuts in any desired path.

2 The coping saw can be used for cutting internal shapes such as large holes. First drill a hole on or near the line to take the saw blade. To insert the blade push the frame against your hip, positioning the wood in the vice accordingly. Loosen the handle by unscrewing it and locate the blade bayonets in their seatings. Tighten up the handle with the blade-holding pin extensions lining up to ensure the blade is not twisted.

Using a powered jigsaw

The jigsaw is a versatile tool for sawing straight and curved work, usually to a line. It is easy to operate once you learn to keep the pressure constantly against the surface of the wood to counteract the upwards snatching of the blade. The jigsaw is capable of removing stock in tight areas such as curves and narrow slits (the bandsaw has a similar capacity).

Using a portable circular saw

1 Circular saws are used for straight cuts across or along the grain and can be set to full or part depth by lowering or raising the blade. The blade can also be adjusted to cut at an angle. You can use the saw to cut 'freehand', using both hands firmly on the handles to control the saw and start the motor before the blade engages with the wood.

2 The standard straight fence can be adjusted to make parallel cuts similar to a router (see Routing, page 60).

3 A clamped batten can serve as a guide for making straight cuts through the wood at any desired position or angle.

Using a track saw

The track saw is a circular saw that clips onto a straight track so that it runs true. The track has non-slip strips on the bottom to stop it from moving. Track saws have a plunging facility, allowing the saw to enter the work at a central point, ideal for cutting sheet material. Lay the track on the line of cut, clip the saw onto the track, plunge the blade and push forwards to make the cut.

Using a chop or mitre saw

1 This portable machine consists of a circular saw blade suspended above a rotating table. It can be used to make extremely accurate crosscuts. With the blade at 90 degrees to the fence, hold the wood against the fence and lower the blade, pushing it towards the fence to make the cut. On a sliding miter saw, you can pull the blade along a sliding arm for cutting wider materials.

2 Both the table and the blade can be swivelled to 45 degrees for cutting mitres. To cut a mitre, rotate the table to the 45-degree mark, position the wood against the fence and make the cut. Alter the angle of the table to cut bevels. For a compound cut, rotate the table and tilt the blade at the same time. If you set both to 45 degrees, you will cut a compound mitre.

3 With some mitre saws, you can adjust the depth of cut. This allows you to cut the two shoulder lines for each side of a housing; you can then remove the waste between them with a series of tightly spaced saw cuts. Use the same procedure for cutting a rebate.

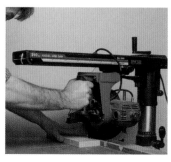

Using a bandsaw

1 A bandsaw is a quiet, efficient machine for cutting both straight and curved work. Its continuous-loop blade passes over two large-diameter wheels. The 'throat' of the bandsaw refers to the distance of the blade to the nearest part of the machine when measured across the table. This determines the length of the piece it can cut across the grain. The wood is supported on the saw's table.

2 Being truly versatile, the bandsaw can cut circles or other curves to a marked line. Make sure your fingers are always away from the blade when supporting and feeding the workpiece. Here the upper blade guide assembly is higher to show the line on the wood and is normally positioned about 25mm (1in) above the wood.

3 The bandsaw is capable of cutting thick pieces of wood. However, this should be done slowly because a bandsaw blade is relatively fragile and also because the waste or sawdust in the cut needs time to clear to avoid overheating. The straight fence on the bandsaw can be used for repeat parallel cuts or for jigging square pieces (see Jigs and Jigmaking, page 63).

Using a radial-arm saw

1 The radial-arm saw is an overhead circular saw; the wood is mounted stationary on the table and the saw head drawn across it. It is primarily used for crosscutting but also for rip, mitre and compound cuts. It has a facility for raising or lowering the saw head for grooves and rebates. The wood is held against the fence and lined up to the saw blade at the marked position for the cut.

Using a table saw

1 A table saw is used for straight cuts along and across the grain. You can raise, lower and tilt the blade. The sliding mitre fence is set to 90 degrees for cutting wood across the grain. You should use both hands to grip the wood against and operate the sliding fence. The clamped block on the rip fence is used for repeat cuts. Safety guard has been lifted for clarity of illustration.

2 The table saw is used for single or repeat cuts along the grain (ripping) and the rip fence is first adjusted and tightened to position before the power is switched on. The riving knife is there to prevent the wood from closing in and jamming the saw cut as the wood passes through. Use push sticks (easily cut on a bandsaw) to guide the wood along and against the fence.

3 The blade can be tilted to cut wood to any angle up to 45 degrees. The sliding fence is used and if set to 45 degrees will facilitate compound mitre cuts.

4 The circular saw blade can be lowered to cut grooves using the rip fence as a guide. Grooves can be widened by adjusting the fence after each cut, and this is particularly useful for cutting the cheeks of tenons. Sometimes a jig is used to secure the wood as it is passed over the blade. Grooved or rebated cuts can be achieved by using the mitre fence with the wood lying the other way.

2 The saw head can be positioned at any angle to make a cut in the crosscut or fixed-head mode by simple adjusting knobs.

3 The rise and fall facility of a radial-arm saw opens up some unique creative possibilities beyond just cutting grooves or rebates. Here a simple 'V' cut jig (see Jigs and Jigmaking, page 63) secures a circular bowl blank (see Turning Wood, page 108) as the saw head is drawn over it to skim the surface perfectly flat.

4 The radial-arm saw can be used for ripping boards down their length. Swing the head around and lock it to the arm, then slightly lower the arm assembly as the blade spins to ensure the blade is fractionally lower than the table surface. The chipboard or MDF saw table is an advantage for jigging, especially when lined with a pinned facing sheet of thin MDF that can take the saw cuts.

5 When ripping it is important to feed the wood in against the rotation of the blades and to first set up the anti-kickback device that prevents the blade from snatching the timber. Guards have been removed for clarity of illustration.

Planing

There is hardly any woodworking that does not include planing somewhere in its process, whether it is smoothing a surface flat, trimming joints true or shaping a piece of wood to a given dimension. Any woodworking novice is likely to use a plane fairly early on, probably at the same time as they learn to use a saw.

The mastery of this age-old tool is highly satisfying, not least because of the sound and smell of the woodshavings passing through the plane body.

Highly accurate planing can be achieved in a fraction of the time with an electric planer-thicknesser, but mastering the basics of hand planing gives you more versatility and a better understanding of the character of wood.

Planes: shapes and sizes

Despite its simple function, the handplane has to be perfectly 'in tune' to perform properly and therefore understanding its mechanics helps.

There are several shapes and sizes of planes. The importance of size (length and weight) is best described by comparing the behaviour of an oil tanker on a rough sea to a small tug on the same sea. The longer plane will cut evenly through the undulations of a wavy board with sufficient weight to give it momentum, whereas a smaller plane will dip into the troughs and be thrown about.

For the beginner the best compromise is a plane that is sufficiently heavy to avoid 'chatter' (the blade not fully engaging with the wood fibres due to lightness) but not so long and heavy as to be cumbersome. A smoothing or small jack plane is therefore the ideal plane for the beginner. There are many makes of planes on the market and they range from junk to masterpieces. It really is worth buying a good one even as a beginner.

Handplane mechanics

The plane blade is basically a wide chisel held in a finely adjusted jig (the plane body). The angle of the blade in the plane body is set (at 45 degrees), the adjusting knob controls the amount of blade protruding through the mouth of the plane and the lever checks that it is cutting parallel across the mouth and therefore not cutting grooves in the wood at one corner of the blade or the other. The plane blade is normally ground to about 25 degrees and its tip sharpened to about 35 degrees (see Tool Maintenance, page 32).

A cap iron is attached to the upper surface of the plane blade with its slightly hooked tip that is positioned 2–3mm (⅛in) from the blade tip. This not only gives reinforcement to the blade tip but causes the shaving to curl over and clear. Each time the blade is sharpened the cap iron has to be removed, so its proper replacement is important.

A well set-up and razor-sharp plane is the vital prerequisite for successful planing. It is well worthwhile familiarising yourself with all the component parts of a plane and knowing their functions. Don't be frightened to take a plane to pieces and have a good look at it. You will learn more doing this yourself than any book can tell you.

A golden rule

There is one golden rule with planing (as with all sharp-edged tools) – the finer the cut, the less resistance of the material and this results in greater control. The action of the handplane is simple. It is held in both hands, one hand to deliver the power and the other hand to apply pressure on to the wood to ensure that the blade bites.

The function of each hand overlaps as the plane travels across the wood, ensuring that contact is made at all times with the blade tip.

CHECKLIST
- **Pencil or ballpoint pen**
- **Sash cramps**
- **Jack plane**
- **Smoothing plane**
- **Electric planer**
- **Health and safety (pages 8–9)**

Using a smoothing or jack plane
1 After sharpening the blade and setting it correctly (see Tool Maintenance, page 32), use a small practice piece of wood mounted in the vice to work out on.

2 Stand in line with the wood, leaning a little into the action (the direction of the cut) as though poised like a boxer with one foot in front of the other for stability.

3 Mark lines across the wood with a pencil or ballpoint pen as 'progress lines' and number equal intervals across the wood. The idea is to plane off in one cut, or 'pass', all three lines at position 1 and work progressively across the workpiece to position 7. The lines indicate whether you are applying pressure consistently from the beginning of the cut to the end. The centre of the plane should be lined up with each mark.

4 As the plane begins its journey, apply more pressure at the nose to keep the blade in perfect contact with the wood fibres. The plane body is in full contact with the wood and the pressure between the hands is consistent, hence maintaining blade tip contact at all times. At the end of the stroke apply more pressure to the heel because the nose of the plane is now no longer in contact with the wood.

5 Constantly adjust and readjust the plane blade to give a controlled cut. If the cut is too thick there will be less control of the plane. You may find you have to turn the wood around the other way to get a 'silky' cut since the grain seldom runs perfectly parallel to the surface. Use a straight-edge to check the wood is flat at regular intervals so that planing and checking for trueness become one skill.

6 When planing it is tempting to slice the plane at an angle. It is true that this will start the cut more easily but there is a danger that you will plane the board out of true because the contact length of the plane's sole (or base) is reduced, and where there is reduced contact over a big area accuracy is lost.

Planing wide boards
Wide boards can be planed diagonally or even across the grain to remove stock quickly and efficiently. This is because fibres are weak across the grain and therefore easily severed. A final smooth finish is achieved by planing with the grain.

Planing an edge 'square' with a smoothing plane

Planing edges is a little more difficult. Planing an edge flat is straightforward but getting it 'square' (90 degrees) takes more practice. If you find you are taking more off one side than the other, use your thumb to line up the centre of the blade with the centre of the wood. Use a try square to check the wood is 90 degrees (see Squaring Wood, page 54).

Planing a chamfer (or angle)

1 Mark chamfers before planing them. An easy way to mark a chamfer is to use the thumb and fingers as a pencil gauge (see Measuring and Marking Out, page 38).

2 Make a series of light plane strokes with the plane held at the appropriate angle. Ideally the wood should be tilted so that the majority of planing is done horizontally. In this way the force of gravity on the plane helps with downward pressure. When holding the plane as shown there is a risk of slippage but with practice this is rarely a problem.

◀ JEREMY BROUN
TABLE
This unusual table is made of solid bubinga, and its construction employs several techniques, including the unusual 'zigzag' joint at the centre. The concept of the three arms of laminated solid strips (planing) that meet in the centre dictates the shape of the jointed intersection, which is cut by careful hand (sawing) and power tool (routing) methods. A stout 'loose' tongue (edge joint) binds the centre joint together. Massive finger joints are used at the corners, and all joints are highlighted with a 1.6mm (1/16in) routed groove.

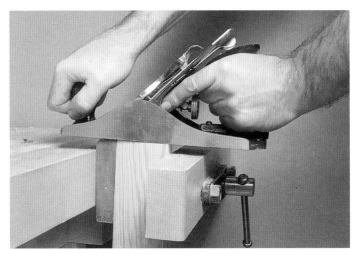

Planing end grain with a smoothing plane

1 End grain will split if the fibres are not supported at the end of the plane stroke. The simplest method is to chisel or plane a small chamfer at the end of the wood, and this you can see just under the front knob of the plane. This ensures the fibres slope away and are not touched by the plane blade, but they remain to give support to the rest of the wood.

2 On wide boards the end grain can be planed first from one direction, then the other. Take care to lift the plane at the end of the halfway stroke to avoid splitting the fibres on the other end. By using this method the end fibres are pushed against the rest of the wood rather than away from it. This then tends to compress them rather than split them out.

3 For shorter end grain work, a supporting block can be made, slightly wedge shaped to fit in the vice or a sash cramp. Take care to ensure the level of the waste piece is flush. If it is too high it will obstruct the plane blade, and if it is too low it will not support the fibres and they will still split out.

Using a portable electric planer

This is a versatile tool for quick stock removal and finishing timber, and it has the advantage of being able to deal with particularly long and heavy boards that would be cumbersome to feed through a planer-thicknesser. Instead the board is stationary and the tool taken to it. Hold the planer firmly because when it is switched on its rotary cutter tends to pull it forwards as it engages with the wood, and this action can be quite vigorous.

1 You will find it best to use both hands and 'skate' the planer along the surface of the wood to maintain even flatness. The depth of cut is set by an adjusting knob that lowers or raises the front part of the planer's soleplate or base.

2 The portable planer is particularly useful for removing stock quickly across the grain. The fibres are weak in this direction and break up easily. Give the piece a final finish with the grain.

3 The portable planer can be upturned and fixed in a purpose-built table, and again these are quite cheap to buy and used as a mini-surface planer. With its fence attached you can 'square' up timber quite easily.

Planing wood using an electric planer-thicknesser

A planer-thicknesser can surface the side and edges of wood (on the top of the machine) and in this mode it is hand fed by the operator, and it can also make the opposite side and edges parallel and flat in the thicknesser (underneath). For this operation it is equipped with automatic feed. It is well worthwhile running a piece of timber back through the machine after it has been planed and thicknessed on both sides completely on automatic feed to eliminate any small ripples. It is in areas such as this that power tools score so heavily over hand methods.

1 First stand towards or astride the machine within easy reach of the start/stop switch and set the feed table height to make a fine cut. Adjust the bridge guard so that the wood can pass underneath it. This is a vital safety precaution as your fingers should never be exposed to the highly rotating cutter block.

2 Switch on the machine and pass the wood over the cutter, holding the wood down at both ends with each hand. The fingers are always on top of the wood except for a minimal finger grip to pull the wood through.

3 As the wood is fed into the cutter, maintain firm downward pressure all the time. 'Walk' the fingers across the bridge guard to maintain the momentum. Some woodworkers prefer to use the palms of their hands for maximum friction grip and ease of operation as the hand passes over the bridge guard. The important factor is safety and keeping fingers well away from the cutter.

Edge planing with an electric planer
1 Set the fence in position and check it is 'square' to the surfacing table. Position the guard so that it covers the cutter up to the board. Feed the timber against the fence. Taking care to avoid the unguarded portion of the cutter block, make a series of light cuts. Check with a square for accuracy and readjust the fence angle if necessary.

2 To plane an angled edge, set the adjustable fence to the desired angle, using a sliding bevel (see Measuring and Marking Out, page 38) and operate as for step 1. Ensure strict contact is made between the wood and the machine surfaces.

Using a thicknesser to make perfectly parallel cuts
1 Check the thickness of the wood and set the thicknessing table to the height of the cut (no more than approximately 1.5mm/¹⁄₁₆in). Feed the wood into the thicknessing table. The automatic feed rollers will engage with the wood and plane the piece. On aluminium-cast machines there is more natural friction between the metal and the wood, so use a little lubricant such as talcum powder to keep the wood moving.

2 Make a series of cuts to the desired dimension, turning the handle a few degrees for each pass. After a while you learn to judge how much to turn each time. The final finish is achieved by turning the wheel a mere fraction.

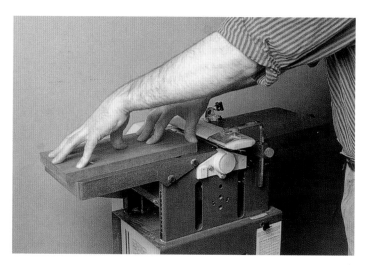

4 The board is passed straight through to the end of the surfacing table. Your stance astride the machine gives equal reach for infeed and outfeed, especially on larger machines. On a smaller machine, such as the one shown here that home woodworkers are most likely to own, this is not necessary. Smaller boards require the use of a push stick (see Jigs and Jigmaking, page 63).

Using a jig

An MDF or melamine-faced board can easily be made up with an end batten screwed on to fix it in place. You can then feed very thin pieces of wood along the tip of the false platform using it as a support. In theory you can plane completely through the board into the platform – so take care to control the cut. Even with the planer blades correctly balanced and razor sharp it is not advisable to cut down to a thickness of board less than 3mm (⅛in). With wild or interlocking grain, there is the risk of fibres breaking as the cutter engages against the grain.

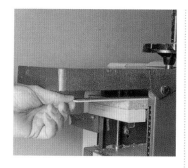

Using the thicknesser to plane tapered or bevelled pieces

1 The false platform can be modified to support triangular-sectioned work by attaching longitudinally the appropriate shaped supporting strips. The work is either rough-sawn first or fed into the thicknesser in rectangular form and reduced in a series of passes to the desired taper. The principle is that the cutter block can only make a parallel cut to the thicknessing table and therefore the wood must go to that shape.

2 The workpiece is lifted from the outfeed end of the thicknesser at the end of its journey. You should take care not to press the wood down because its release from the rear guide rollers as it comes past them can force the end of the wood back up into the cutter block and this will then cut off more than is required. It is interesting to note here that even when using power tools as opposed to hand tools some degree of skill is still involved.

Squaring Wood

Woodworking depends on accuracy, which usually means working to a line – it is important to make sure the wood is accurately prepared to size beforehand. This technique is called 'preparation of timber' or 'squaring'.

When timber has been bought rough-sawn or even pre-planed it requires squaring, not least of all because there are likely to be twists or bows, especially in softwoods that are not fully seasoned.

A piece of timber has been squared when all surfaces are flat, adjacent surfaces are 90 degrees to each other and opposite surfaces are parallel. You may find it necessary, when making a table for instance, to prepare accurately four identical pieces for the legs and a series of identical pieces to edge-joint the top together (see cutting lists in Drawing, page 36). Hence the need for a standard squaring procedure.

The full procedure is achieved by either hand or power tools, the latter being far quicker. You will find it is an advantage to practise the hand process first, however painstaking, as such difficulty leads to a full appreciation of the need for skill and accuracy.

CHECKLIST
- **Steel rule**
- **Marking knife**
- **Pencil or ballpoint pen**
- **Marking gauge**
- **Try square**
- **Tenon or dovetail saw**
- **Smoothing or jack plane**
- **Planer-thicknesser**
- **Circular saw or radial-arm saw or bandsaw or jigsaw**
- **Health and safety (pages 8–9)**

Squaring timber by hand
1 Select the best side (face side) and plane it flat and smooth (see Planing, page 48). Hold the work on the benchtop using dogs or stops, checking with a straight-edge or rule. Mark the first side with a face side mark that extends to the best edge (face edge). Face marks are important when gauging or using a square; the stock is normally placed against the face side or face edge.

6 Square to length using a try square, steel rule and marking knife. First set the zero of the steel rule against one end of the timber and measure in about 6mm (¼in). This is the minimum amount of wood that can be easily cut off with a tenon saw. Now move the steel rule so that the zero lines up with the 6mm (¼in) mark and measure off the required length (leaving at least 6mm/¼in).

7 You should use the try square with its stock against the face edge. Locate the marking knife in the first mark, slide the try square up to it and mark a line carefully across. Locating the knife in the previous cut line, square the line all the way around the timber, keeping the stock of the try square against either face side or face edge. This is important to ensure the lines will meet up.

8 Shade in the waste with a pencil or ballpoint pen ready for cutting the ends off. Using a bench-hook mounted in the vice saw off the ends with a tenon saw on the waste side of the line.

9 Finally, if necessary, trim the end grain with a plane. Take care to avoid splitting the end grain by using a supporting block in the vice.

2 Mount the wood low in the vice and plane the face edge square (90 degrees) to the face side. Check the accuracy with a try square and steel rule. Mark the face edge mark so it adjoins the face side mark.

3 A marking gauge is set to gauge to width. Use it vertically with the spur touching the appropriate calibration on the steel rule. Now mount the wood at an angle in the vice and carefully gauge to width, trailing the spur at a shallow angle and ensuring the stock is kept firmly against the face edge. Mark a line all the way around the wood.

4 Shade the waste portion and then mount the timber in the vice and plane to width. As you approach the line adjust the plane to cut a fine shaving. Almost as the marking gauge line is reached a fine sliver of wood can be easily rubbed away at each edge, indicating that only a few fine plane strokes are required to reach the line. In theory the edge should be perfectly square.

5 Check the minimum thickness of the wood and set the marking gauge, this time to gauge the thickness. Now gauge to thickness a line all the way around the wood. With a little practice you can quickly gauge holding the timber freehand. Plane to thickness, taking care to constantly check the line after a few plane strokes.

Squaring timber by machine
1 First cut the timber slightly oversize as straight as possible – length + 25mm (1in) width + 6mm (¼in) thickness + 2–3mm (⅛in). Using a planer-thicknesser surface plane the face side, making a few passes until it is flat (see Planing, page 48). Make sure the bridge guard is in place and pass your hands over it as you push the wood through. Pencil a face side mark on the planed side.

2 Now set the fence at 90 degrees and plane the face edge square and true. Pencil a face edge mark on to the edge.

3 Set the thicknessing table to the width of the piece of wood and feed in the piece. A few passes will be required, adjusting the cut with the hand wheel.

4 Finally, set the thicknessing table to the thickness of the wood and feed in the wood to reduce in stages to the desired dimension. If the board is wide, use a steel rule and marking knife, ballpoint pen or pencil to mark a parallel line. Shade in the waste and plane down to the line. Measure the precise length required and mark with a pencil, then saw off using a circular saw, radial-arm saw etc.

Chiselling

Like sawing, chiselling is an essential woodworking skill. It is primarily a hand technique requiring some degree of dexterity, which with practice you will soon acquire. The hand chisel is used for cutting, trimming and shaping, and in particular for removing stock or waste in joint cutting.

Powered chiselling (mortising) generally refers to the use of a purpose-built hollow chisel mortiser or an attachment to the power drill that cuts rectangular slots out of the wood. It combines the action of an auger drill and a square-edged chisel, which is pressed with force into the workpiece.

In general this method is found more in industrial workshops, and the powered mortiser is certainly not a necessity for the home enthusiast. This method is usually applied to cutting mortises (see Mortise and Tenon Joints, page 90).

Common to all chiselling is the design of the chisel blade. This is bevelled or sloped to a razor-sharp edge that has to be kept keen (see Tool Maintenance, page 32).

There are two bevels: the ground angle (approximately 25 degrees), in which condition the tool is normally bought; and the sharpened angle (approximately 30 degrees). The sharpened

angle is put on using an oilstone or something similar in your own workshop. Chisels do vary in action, and a shallower ground or sharpened blade slices through the wood more easily than a steeper angled chisel, although the latter is stronger. Types of chisels vary from bevel-edged (which in this case means that the sides of the chisel are sloped also, but not sharpened); firmer (square-edged for some joint cutting); and mortise chisels (which are stouter and can be levered in and out of the wood).

Hand chiselling takes some practice, but done well, it is very rewarding.

CHECKLIST
- **Marking tools**
- **Bevel-edged and/or firmer or mortise chisels**
- **Mortising attachment for drill or hollow chisel mortiser**
- **Set of chisel bits (6, 9, 12mm/ ¼, ⅜, ½in)**
- **Health and safety (pages 8–9)**

Working across the grain
1 The chisel can be used efficiently to sever fibres across the grain; a little help with a mallet is needed here. A general rule is that when cutting a mortise or similar square recess, the fibres are cut across the grain first to avoid splitting.

2 After the fibres have been severed across the grain, you can then chisel down the grain without the fibres splitting. A series of cuts to loosen the fibres precedes the final cut to the line.

3 With both hands behind the chisel's cutting edge, one hand is used to deliver the power and the other to guide the chisel. The guiding hand is crucial for control and here the fingers squeeze tightly around the chisel blade and the forefinger rests against the edge of the work, acting as a depth-stop.

Narrow chisels vs wide chisels
Experience will show that more cutting control is achieved with a narrow chisel than with a wide one, as there is less resistance from the wood fibres. Chisels vary in width from about 3mm (⅛in) to 38mm (1½in). A bevel-edged 9mm (⅜in) or 12mm (½in) chisel is a good size to use for general work.

Working along the grain
1 The fibrous nature of wood lends itself to the action of the chisel, which by its wedge-shaped section slices into the wood, separating the fibres along the grain. Hold the chisel firmly, with both hands behind the cutting edge.

2 Here the chisel is held like a dagger for overhead paring, which means cutting along the grain. The guiding fingers and thumb give excellent control for taking off the exact amount of wood. The chisel is frequently used in conjunction with the saw, and here the saw has been used to sever the fibres across the grain first.

3 Alternatively you can chisel away the waste by holding the wood horizontally. Depending on the grain character of the wood, you might find it easier to cut across the grain first and then finish to the line with the grain, or vice versa. It depends on how the grain wants to behave. In any event you should always work to a marked line.

Forming curves
Although there are quicker ways to form curves (see Shaping Wood, page 101), the chisel can be used to radius (curve) a corner, paring a series of fine flat cuts.

Using a mortise chisel
1 The mortise chisel is strong enough to lever against the wood, helping with the removal of chippings.

2 A series of cuts across the grain breaks the wood up into small chippings. You will find these are easy to remove when cutting a typical feature such as a hinge recess (see Hinges and Locks, page 120).

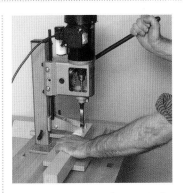

Powered chiselling (mortising)
1 A hollow chisel mortiser is easy to use once the workpiece has been aligned and clamped. Be sure to spend time in getting this right – it is a very important part of the job.

2 A series of square holes is cut to make a mortise. The auger bit cuts a hole and the square-bodied, sharp-edged chisel housing is pressed into the wood, making a clean square-edged cut.

Drilling

The technique of drilling accurately is one of the first things to learn in the workshop. Modern methods have made this considerably easier.

Holes are 'drilled' by the removal of wood fibres with an 'Archimedes-screw'-type bit that is rotated at speed in the chuck of a hand or power drill. The fibres are severed and cleared from the hole by the drill flutings or grooves.

Holes can also be cut by the scraping action of a flat or spade bit that is specifically designed for a power drill. Hand-drilling has been largely superseded by the more efficient power drill, which can be hand-held or fixed in a drill stand.

Power drilling

The portable electric drill gave birth to the power-tool revolution. Early power-tool attachments for the drill included jigsaws, circular saws (see Sawing, page 44) and sanders (see Abrading, page 104). There is hardly a workshop without a portable drill. These adaptable machines can be easily mounted into a vertical drill stand for precise and accurate drilling on the bench.

Most drills are mains operated with keyed chucks for gripping the bit firmly. They are rated by wattage (average 500 watts) and chuck capacity 10–13mm (⅜–½in), which refers to the maximum size of bit that can be fitted. The advantage of modern flat bits is that wide holes, up to 38mm (1½in), can be achieved from a 6mm (¼in) shank diameter.

Less torque (twisting power) is required to operate flat bits but purists argue that they tear wood fibres rather than cleanly cut them and the twist drill is preferred for general accuracy. However, twist drills are liable to wander in the wood, especially in end grain, and it is preferable to use a wood-bit that has a defined centre point.

Drilling pilot holes

For drilling small pilot holes (see Hinges and Locks, page 120) a tiny twist bit is used because flat bits are seldom available in diameters less than 6mm (¼in). You can of course profile or shape your own flat bits using a bench grinder (see Tool Maintenance, page 32).

Cordless or battery-operated portable drills are popular, although they are less powerful than mains-operated drills. They offer convenience in and out of the workshop. Being low voltage (3.6–24 volts), cordless power tools are safer electrically.

Recharging of batteries can be achieved in as little as five minutes and it always pays to carry spares. These drills are handy for working a long way from a power supply and, from a safety point of view, for working in wet conditions.

The keyed chuck has been replaced to a large extent by the keyless chuck, which offers adequate grip to the drill bit. Such drills with their torque-adjusted clutches can double up as powered screwdrivers.

There are numerous attachments that will fit into power drills, ranging from hinge-sinking cutters to rotary rasps and abrading discs.

CHECKLIST
- **Power drill (hammer action not vital)**
- **Power drill stand**
- **Set of twist bits**
- **Set of flat bits**
- **Countersink bit**
- **Health and safety (pages 8–9)**

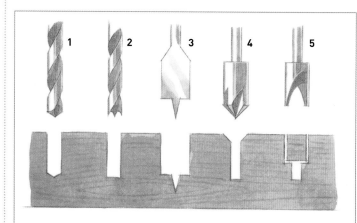

SELECTION OF TWIST DRILLS AND FLAT BITS

1 Twist bit for making small holes; also useful for waste clearance and starting screws.

2 Dowelling bit for setting wooden dowels needing a square-bottomed hole.

3 Flat bit works with a scraping action; cuts large holes rapidly.

4 The countersink bit is to allow a screw head to lie flush with the work's surface.

5 The plug cutter removes waste in one piece to allow it to be replaced later.

How to use a hand-held power drill

1 Insert the required drill bit into the chuck, making sure it is tightened with the key in all three holes.

2 When marking positions for drilling holes, a cross is generally used to denote the centre. For end grain drilling it is preferable to use a drill bit that has a clearly defined centre point.

3 Clasp your hands around the drill comfortably, positioning yourself above the workpiece, and locate the drill bit and commence drilling. Occasionally withdraw the drill bit in order to clear the chippings, which have a tendency to clog and overheat.

4 When drilling straight-through holes it is important to stop drilling when the point of the flat bit appears through the wood, then turn the workpiece around and drill from the other side; this is to prevent splitting or what is known as 'breakout'.

Using a drill stand

1 Install the drill into the drill stand, making sure it is secure. Insert the correct bit, using the chuck key to secure it.

2 Place scrapwood underneath the workpiece for straight-through holes. For blind holes (holes that do not go all the way through) you will need to set the depth-stop on the drill stand. Carefully hold down the workpiece with one hand, anticipating the rotary snatching of the drill bit (especially wide-diameter flat bits). Switch on the power with your other hand and gently lower the bit into the wood.

3 Countersunk holes (for sinking the screw head level with the surface of the wood, or deeper) can be achieved by setting the depth-stop.

Routing

The electric plunging router is almost unprecedented as a modern woodworking tool because of its enormous creative potential. It is basically a high-speed (8,000-25,000 rpm) electric motor driving a spindle; the spindle carries a collet (a type of chuck) into which a sharp-edged rotating cutter is inserted. Some routers are variable speed with a soft start.

The router's simplest function is to convert a hole into a groove by plunging the cutter into the wood and drawing the tool via its adjustable fence across the timber. When you extend the range of cutters to include profiled shapes, and then expand the function of the fence, which serves as a guiding jig, by using other types of jigging device, the router does not stop at just cutting grooves and rebates. It can profile edges, cut through wood to any shape, cut joints, trim wood flat, make screw threads and much more. Despite its simplicity of concept the router is a precise and sophisticated shaping tool. The three main elements of routing are: the size of the router, the variety of cutters and the types of jigging devices.

Router sizes

Routers vary in motor power, ranging from 500–1100 watts (up to 1.5 horsepower) for smaller routers and up to 3000 watts (4 horsepower) for larger ones. Within these sizes are different collet options, with both imperial and metric sizing

being used. The most common collet size is ¼in for smaller routers and ½in for larger ones. Other collet sizes include 6mm, 8mm, ⅜in and 12mm. Larger routers can take smaller collets, but small routers cannot take large collets. Being lighter, a smaller router can be a good choice for a beginner; a soft start router would be a bonus.

Cutter size

Cutters are available in different shank diameters to fit each collet size. Imperial and metric cutters are not interchangeable – a 6mm shank diameter will be too loose to fit into a ¼in (6.35mm) collet and is unsafe. Although the range of cutters is greater in larger and stronger shank sizes, routing creativity does not rely on numerous cutters: a handful of basic profiles can be used for a variety of purposes. Cutters are generally tungsten-carbide tipped steel (TCT) and should be stored in a protective container.

CHECKLIST
- **Small, medium or large router with appropriate collet sleeves**
- **Straight fence and wheel fence**
- **Guide bush(es) and selection of cutters (see box, right)**
- **Batten and 'G' clamps**
- **MDF template material**
- **Double-sided tape**
- **Router table**
- **Drill stand with 43mm (1⅝in) collar**
- **Health and safety (pages 8–9)**

Jigging devices

The most basic jigging device is the adjustable straight fence that is attached to the router. It is used for straight grooves and rebates parallel to the edge of the wood. The fence can also be used for cutting mortises and tenons (see page 90). Other jigs include the roller guide, which allows parallel cuts to be made to a concave or convex edge, and a variety of guide bushes that are used against shaped templates.

CUTTER TYPES AND GUIDE BUSH APPLICATION

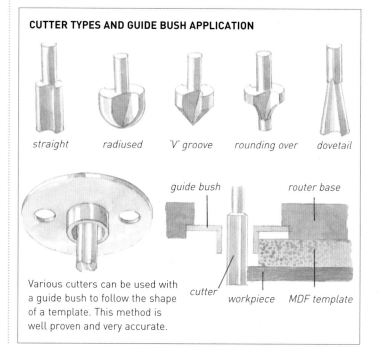

straight   *radiused*   *'V' groove*   *rounding over*   *dovetail*

guide bush   *router base*

cutter   *workpiece*   *MDF template*

Various cutters can be used with a guide bush to follow the shape of a template. This method is well proven and very accurate.

Setting up

Cutters are fragile and expensive. Most new cutters are protected in an oiled plastic coating that you need to peel off. Loosen the collet nut on the router, insert the cutter and tighten the nut. The shaft will have some form of locking device to aid this – either a locking nut and additional spanner or a press lock above the collet.

First steps in freehand routing

1 To get the 'feel' of a router try freehand routing shallow grooves (a simple name plaque is a good first exercise). First set the cutter to depth using the depth-stop. A golden rule is to cut in depth no more than half the diameter of the cutter in one pass (stroke).

2 It is important that the power switch is within finger reach. With the router switched off, position the cutter where you want to plunge the first cut. Now switch on and firmly but slowly plunge into the wood to the depth-stop. As you do this, start the horizontal movement, passing the router freehand over the marked line. Keep the cutter moving.

3 At the end of the stroke release the plunge lock (either untwist the hand grip or use the plunge-locking lever) and the cutter will spring back up. You can see that in this simple freehand exercise keeping to the line is not crucial, but it offers excellent practice in controlling the tool. Try to avoid burn marks.

Template routing using a guide bush

1 Creative routing can be achieved by using a guide bush as a spacer between the cutter and a template for grooving and edge trimming. The guide bush is a lipped collar that is screwed into the router base. There is a variety of diameter lips relating to different cutter diameters. The general rule is to coordinate a measurement of 2–3mm (⅛in) between cutter edge and lip edge.

2 Use double-sided tape to fix the MDF template on to the slightly oversize workpiece. 'G' clamps can be used but they have to be moved around to allow the router to pass. A long straight cutter is used here to finish a rough-sawn edge perfectly smooth and square. The guide bush makes contact with the MDF template and a series of cuts progressively works through to full depth. For such long cutters a large-capacity router is usually required.

Using a router head in the drill stand

1 Simple drilling or milling (horizontal grooves) can be achieved with some routers with a standard 43mm (1⅝in) collar. This router is released from its plunging/base assembly. It is inserted into the matching 43mm (1⅝in) collar of a drill stand and tightened.

2 The router can be used for drilling much cleaner holes than a normal twist bit or flat bit, but you have to be careful to avoid burning the wood as the debris has to escape. This drill stand has a tilting head that makes the router even more versatile for special jigged operations, including dowelling at an angle (see Dowel Joints, page 80).

Using the straight fence

The straight fence is supplied with the router as standard kit and it can be adjusted to width to rout grooves, rebates and edge profiles such as chamfers (using a 'V' cutter). You will need to attach a wooden facing strip to the fence because for this and other operations a cutaway is required in the fence. It is common practice for woodworkers to make up their own wooden fences for routers and indeed for other tools such as circular saws.

To cut a simple chamfer, set the cutter to depth, lock the plunge mechanism and draw the router along the wood, keeping the fence in strict contact with the edge, just like a marking gauge (see Measuring and Marking Out, page 38).

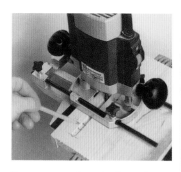

Two screws adjust the fence for cutting grooves. This stopped groove is simply marked first and the groove is cut in steps by a series of 'passes'. You can see the three stages by which the groove is being executed. This maximises the life of the cutter and does not overload a small router. It is good practice to take several small cuts rather than one large one.

Batten routing

By securing a straight-edge on to the workpiece using 'G' clamps a versatile jig can be made. When calculating where to place the batten in relation to the desired cut, the crucial measurement is taken from the edge of the router base to the cutter. Straight, 'V' grooved or radiused cutters can be used to make different profiled cuts. Apply firm pressure towards the batten.

Using a router table

1 Most routers fix into a proprietary table, converting the tool into a mini-spindle moulder. The position and height of the cutter are fixed and the wood passed over the table surface against the appropriate jig. In this case a straight fence and straight cutter are being used to form a rebate. Press the wood firmly into the base/fence as it passes over the cutter, keeping fingers well clear.

2 The router table is set up with a wheel guide for profiling convex and concave work. Here a radiused edge is being cut. The final finish is achieved with abrasive paper (see Abrading, page 104).

Cutting a tenon using the router

1 A straight fence and straight cutter are used. Two marks are made on the wood to indicate the settings of the straight fence and the depth of cutter. To set the fence to the correct width place the router with its cutter lowered to just above the wood surface. Set the depth-stop to the vertical mark.

2 Work the router along the edge by first setting to half depth and cutting back to the shoulder (up to the fence). Set the depth-stop to full depth of cut and work the router across, taking great care to keep the router sole flat against the wood and not tilt it so the cutter cuts below the intended path. Now reverse the wood and cut the other tenon cheek.

Jigs and Jigmaking

A jig is a device used to hold or guide the workpiece while it is being worked on or to hold or guide the tool being used, often for repeat actions. The craft of woodworking becomes an art when you start making your own jigs.

Once you have acquired the basic woodworking techniques of measuring, sawing, chiselling, planing and so on, and can make joints fit first time (see Jointing Principles, page 70), you will soon see that much woodworking is either based on repeat operations (such as fashioning identical members)

or dealing with awkward 'one-off' problems that standardised equipment and methods do not readily solve.

Behind the art of jigmaking is the ability to improvise, and for many trained woodworkers it often means putting aside a rather rigid doctrine and thinking 'laterally', using whatever means are available. Jigs can be very simple or sometimes really quite complex. They are usually the brainchild of the individual and more often than not are quite simple solutions for very specific applications.

This might mean the use of pins and nails, adhesive tape, a hot-melt glue gun (as an extra pair of hands), offcuts of plywood, chipboard and MDF, and quick solidifying materials such as car body filler.

Certain hand and power tools require jigs for specific tasks, either to make the task easier or quicker.

CHECKLIST
- **MDF, chipboard or plywood**
- **Softwood**
- **Hot-melt glue gun**
- **Screws, nails, pins**
- **Masking tape**
- **A range of hand tools**
- **A range of power tools**
- **Health and safety (pages 8–9)**

Some basic jigs for hand tools
1 A custom-built saw guide is used here for cutting dovetail housings. A stout block of wood is sawn and planed accurately and when 'G' clamped to the workpiece it acts as a guide for the saw blade. Care has to be taken in aligning the jig perfectly with the wall of the housing.

2 An angled block can help maintain a consistent and accurate cut when chiselling the corresponding piece to a dovetailed housing joint.

3 Similarly a square-edged hardwood block can be used for trimming the shoulder lines of a dovetail with a chisel. The block should be clamped perfectly in line with the shoulder line and the chisel pressed firmly against the vertical wall of the block.

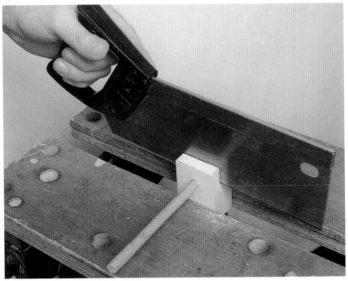

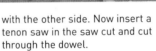

Using a dowel-cutting jig
1 One of the simplest workshop jigs to make is this dowel-cutting device – a small block of wood with a hole, a saw cut and a nail partially buried.

2 First, support the jig in the vice. Bevel the end of a piece of dowel and push it through until it is flush with the other side. Now insert a tenon saw in the saw cut and cut through the dowel.

3 Using a hammer, drive the dowel through the end. As it passes against the nail point, a groove is formed that acts as an air-escape channel in the dowel joint. This also allows excess glue to escape.

Simple power-tool jigs
1 The bandsaw (see Sawing, page 44) is an ideal powered tool for jigging up. The most basic jig is its standard straight fence, which can be used for parallel repeat cuts along or down the grain.

2 Saw kerfing can be achieved easily on the bandsaw by mounting a straight-edged scrap piece on the saw table with 'G' clamps so that the blade is half buried in a saw cut. This acts as a sawing depth-stop. With a push stick you can make a series of cuts, aligning the previous cut with a mark on the straight piece of equal spacing.

3 The router is perhaps the most versatile power tool for work with jigs (see Routing, page 60). Indeed the router body is a jig for guiding the path of the cutter. Here is a simple method of trimming the ends of dovetail or finger joints. Attach a thin piece of ply or MDF to the joint piece with masking tape or 'G' clamps.

4 Position the MDF just behind the shoulder line of the dovetails. The MDF serves as a spacer for accurately setting the depth of the cutter to the surface of the wood while operating the router sole against the MDF.

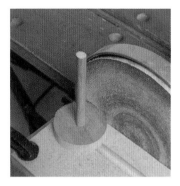

A simple wheel-cutting device
1 This simple device – designed by the author – is used to cut accurate wheels for toys or other small circular sections that require a centre hole. It comprises a block of wood with a groove cut into it. It is mounted on to a disc sander table.

2 An oversize 'wheel' is roughly cut on the bandsaw and its spindle fits loosely in the groove. As the wheel is rotated against the abrading disc, pressure of the dowel spindle is increased against the inside wall of the groove.

3 First a small 'flat' is sanded against the marked circle on the wheel, which is cut slightly oversize.

4 Insert the wheel with its spindle protruding into the groove against the outer edge of the groove. Using finger control, slowly rotate the wheel so that it makes contact with the sanding disc and abrades gradually to the line. Take care not to catch your fingers on the sanding disc as it rotates. Any number of wheels can be made; have a go at it!

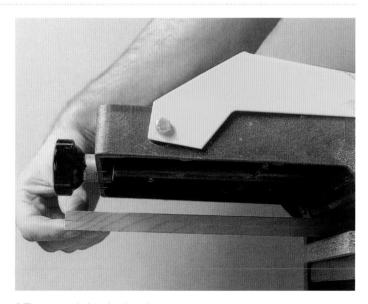

Jigmaking materials
MDF, chipboard, a hot-melt glue gun and pins or screws are ideal partners for jigmaking. You can quickly build custom jigs that need only be as permanent as the job in hand.

Making a jig for the planer-thicknesser
1 A taper channel is constructed by gluing and pinning the corresponding waste pieces on to the chipboard. A batten underneath secures the jig to the thicknessing table.

2 The tapered piece is planed down in the thicknesser in stages until the required taper is formed.

Gluing

Most items of woodwork rely on glue to hold them together. Very few wood joints or wood components stay together solely by mechanical means, unless they are specifically designed to do so (as in the case of 'knockdown furniture' or some very intricate Japanese joints). The mortise and tenon, for example, was originally a dry joint and was held together by adding pins.

Until quite recenty, glues were liable to degrade over a period of time, causing furniture to fall apart; today the notion of a 'permanent' bond is as familiar in woodworking as it is in metalworking, where epoxy glues are often used instead of welds. Modern woodworking glues are stronger than the surrounding wood fibres, and when something breaks it is unlikely to be along the glue line. A popular type of glue for its strength, open time and clamping time is aliphatic resin, which is a type of PVA glue.

Gluing up can vary in complexity from the relatively simple gluing of a 'rubbed' joint (two pieces glued edge to edge and slid against each other to form a suction) to the gluing and clamping of numerous parts of a carcase.

Gluing usually requires constant pressure throughout the curing period and hence gluing and clamping is an integral process and a vital stage in the making of a piece of woodwork.

Careful preparation is required to avoid disastrous results, and usually a 'dry run' is executed to check that clamps and other equipment are immediately at hand and set to position.

CHECKLIST
- PVA glue
- Urea-formaldehyde glue
- Water
- Spatula
- Cloth
- 'G' clamps and sash cramps
- Epoxy resin glue
- Methylated spirit or acetone
- Health and safety (pages 8–9)

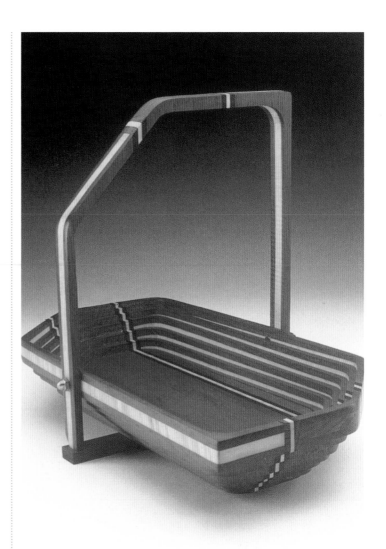

▲ DEEP SPRING STUDIO
BASKET
What is not immediately evident from the photograph is that this basket is collapsible. Different woods – padauk, ebony and tiger maple – are laid in sequence and laminated and edge-glued to form a solid block about 25mm (1in) deep. The handle is cut first, and then the body is cut in a continuously decreasing spiral. When the piece is folded flat, therefore, the pattern of the grain and lamination appears as a complete design over the entire surface. All the cutting is carried out with a bandsaw used freehand. The basket is opened up by, first, gently raising the sides and then by carefully rotating the handle into position.

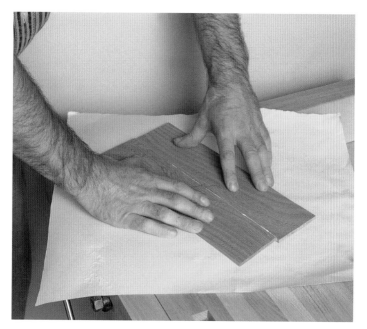

2 Against a flat surface (such as the bench protected with paper), use a sliding motion to rub both pieces vigorously. This squeezes out the glue and creates a suction. There is no need for clamps. Leave the panel to dry for 2 hours in a warm environment.

Gluing a 'rubbed' joint

1 The essence of this simple joint for thin boards is in the accurate planing of the two contact surfaces (see Planing, page 48, and Squaring Wood, page 54). After this has been checked, apply PVA glue to one surface and spread it out evenly.

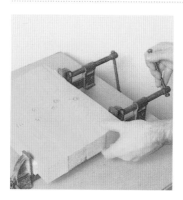

Gluing a stack-laminated panel

1 After accurately preparing the separate pieces of wood to size, mount them in two sash cramps to check their alignment. This is called a 'dry run' and is essential for most glue-and-clamp operations. You can number the pieces with location marks to ensure perfect alignment.

2 Arrange the glue-contact edges uppermost and apply PVA swiftly to each piece in turn. Locate each piece to the coded marks, applying the glue with a spatula. If the work is large use a longer-drying synthetic glue rather than PVA, which only allows 2 or 3 minutes working time.

3 Use a hammer and scrapwood to align the pieces before the final clamping pressure is applied.

4 It is likely the wood will 'wander' a little under pressure, in which case slacken off the cramps and realign the wood. When the pieces are finally clamped, wipe off excessive glue with a damp cloth.

Gluing and clamping frameworks using sash cramps

1 Use scrapwood blocks with the cramps to prevent bruising or marking. To maintain squareness, align the centre of the cramp with the centre of the thickness of the wood.

2 Check with a try square and move the cramps fractionally to adjust squareness if this should be necessary.

3 For checking to see if frameworks (and carcases) are square, a diagonal rod can be used to check the opposing internal dimensions. These must of course be exactly the same.

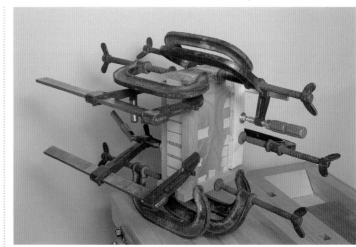

Epoxy 'fillet' bonding

1 Epoxy resins are two-part adhesives (resin and hardener) and should be mixed to the manufacturer's specification. Epoxies are extremely strong; their added strength allows 'fillet' bonding, whereby thin material can be reinforced by the epoxy running into the corner. After applying the resin, tilt the structure so that the resin flows along the joint.

2 To make the adhesive easier to apply, microfibre filler or colloidal silica can be mixed into the resin (after the hardener has been mixed). A slightly thicker mix prevents over-absorption of the glue around the joint area. Thicker mixes can be used when joint accuracy is not crucial and the resin acts as a filler-glue, or when using a spatula to 'feather' the fillet on right-angle bends in thin materials.

Gluing a small carcase

The carcase is comprised of four sides with a top and base – a lot of clamping! It can be clamped in stages (for example, the body first) or achieved in one go, using masking tape for initial alignment of the pieces. Virtually all available space has been taken up by 'G' clamps. This happens often in clamping, which only emphasises the need for good preparation as all gluing is done 'against the clock'.

Gluing a dovetail joint
1 A dovetail joint has an extended gluing contact area and it is best to use a glue – such as urea formaldehyde – with a longer pot life. First check the joint fits 'dry'.

2 Mix up the glue with the powder and then add small amounts of water – never the other way round. Allow 4 parts glue to 1 part water.

3 To avoid lumps mix a thick paste and thin it with water gradually.

4 When the glue runs off like treacle it is correctly mixed. Leave it to stand for a few minutes. The pot life of urea-formaldehyde is about 10–20 minutes, after which it thickens and becomes unusable.

5 Using a wooden spatula, thinly apply the glue to both surfaces.

6 Tap the joint together using a hammer and scrapwood along the shoulder line.

7 Then place the scrapwood in between the joint fingers and gently hammer down to make good shoulder line contact.

8 A cutaway clamping block should be used to allow for the slight joint protrusion. Check for squareness with a try square, and leave the whole assembly to cure for at least 8 hours.

Jointing Principles

Jointing is at the very heart of woodworking. It is, arguably, the most important technique to learn as well as being a satisfying experience when done well. Most woodworking consists of joining pieces of wood together for a variety of purposes – be it for changing shape, creating structure, maximising strength or dealing with timber movement.

There is the decorative aspect, too: when two pieces of wood join they create immense visual interest (sometimes even mystery).

There are hundreds of joints in existence. Many have evolved over the centuries to meet specific functional requirements, such as the mortise and tenon and dovetail joints in frame and carcase construction. As such, joints embody a rich and long-standing wood culture, and just as a particular timber such as oak spans entire centuries and thus has strong historical associations, so too do particular wood joints, most notably the dovetail.

Joints and timber movement

Not least in importance in the vast vocabulary of wood joints is the behaviour of wood itself, namely timber movement. This is something all woodworkers must reckon with because nature will get its way.

Timber is like a sponge, absorbing, holding and losing moisture from the air. All joints therefore move to a degree and their geometry and dimensions are crucial factors in restricting or coping with timber movement. A well-designed joint is strong, visually attractive or cleverly hidden and, above all, survives the passage of time, when constant shrinking and swelling of the fibres affect its structure.

A simple rule is that timber tends to move across the grain rather than along the grain and the annual rings (visible on end grain) will try to straighten out. Therefore care should be taken to select timber that is quarter sawn (with short annual rings across the board section); this will minimise timber movement.

Modern 'permanent' adhesives have given a degree of freedom in jointing methods. A thin veneer glued down with a modern glue is unlikely to shrink out and split, but a thick panel glued to another with incorrect grain intersections will move. It is not the glue line that breaks but the wood fibres around it.

Jointing manufactured boards

Manufactured boards such as chipboard and MDF are less prone to timber movement, and hence employ a different variety of connecting methods. Board materials anyway have little localised mechanical strength and break away at the edges if traditional solid wood joints are used.

These materials exploit modern machine jointing methods such as grooved fillets or designated finger joint cutters (see Edge Joints, page 78). The subject of jointing man-made boards is very wide and it would be safe to say that if your particular interest in woodworking lies in this field further reading will be necessary.

The principles of wood jointing

There is nothing more satisfying than to cut a tight joint, as it demands not only an understanding of the nature of the material but a good command of technique with a keen eye and sustained concentration. Some understanding of the principles of wood jointing helps before acquiring the 'knacks' of how to make a tight joint. A basic rule is to avoid short grain. If a joint is cut too close to the end of a piece of wood and the fibres are severed deeper across the grain than along it, the stress of the joint and any leverage bearing upon it will result in the 'short grain' breaking along the grain.

COMMON JOINTS
- **Butt joint:** simple carcases; useful if no strength is needed.
- **Half lap joint:** for joining timber of the same section at an angle.
- **Tongue and groove:** for joining boards edgeways; useful in panelling.
- **Spline joint:** like tongue and groove but with a loose spline.
- **Mortise and tenon:** one of the most common framing joints; consists of a square hole with a square peg in it.
- **Dovetail:** comes in many forms, some hidden; common in carcase and drawer making; often used overtly to show quality and craftsmanship.
- **Scarf:** used to join two pieces of timber lengthways; often used in shipbuilding.
- **Dowel joint:** an easy alternative to the mortise and tenon; can be surprisingly difficult to align; useful in cabinet making.
- **Biscuit joint:** used mainly for edge jointing but also in other areas.
- **Domino joint:** a robust joint, often used as a substitute for a mortise and tenon.
- **Mitre:** popular with picture framers, cabinet makers etc; invariably needs reinforcement of some kind.

X–Y SHORT GRAIN RULE ON JOINTS

When cutting a joint close to the end of a piece of wood, the depth of the cut ('X') must not exceed the length of the piece remaining on the end ('Y'). If it does, this short grain will certainly break. This is because the pressure or leverage to which the joint is subjected is too great for the short grain over the reduced area.

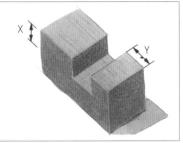

Principles of wood jointing – a basic guide

1 An end grain to end grain glue joint (see Gluing, page 66) is the weakest as there is no fibre overlap and the glue is absorbed down the grain, leaving too little on the mating surfaces.

2 An end grain to side grain glue joint is almost as weak as an end grain to end grain glue joint (see step 1) for the same reasons, and also because the wood will shrink across the grain and stress the glue line.

3 The strongest glue joint occurs when two similar grain directions meet side by side, in effect continuing the figure of the wood. When shrinkage occurs it is consistent as both pieces behave in the same way (see Edge Joints, page 78).

4 By introducing a shoulder to the joint it becomes mechanically stronger and the principle of strong jointing is to create maximum fibre overlap and maximum glue area. Here you can see the dovetail and finger joints are mechanically strong. They also offer great visual interest.

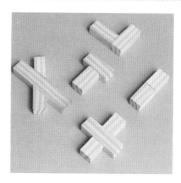

Types of joint configuration

1 There are basically four jointing configurations to be found in wood constructions: 'L', 'T', 'X' and 'I'. There are also oblique or angled variations of these types. Each configuration can be achieved by a variety of joints. For instance the 'L' type can be a halving joint, a mitre joint, a bridle joint, a dowel joint, a dovetail joint or a mortise and tenon. Hence the family of joints is extensive.

2 This is the simplest 'L' joint, in which one piece overlaps the other with adjacent grain and the glue bond is reasonably strong. Such a joint could alternatively be nailed or screwed together. It can be made stronger by setting one piece into the other, creating a shoulder that helps lock the two pieces together. When the shoulder is cut halfway through the thickness of each piece, a halving joint results that is the strongest type of glued 'L' joint.

3 Above left is an 'L' mitre joint, and to the right of it you can see that the same two pieces of wood can be rearranged to form other joint types – an oblique scarf joint and a normal scarf joint (both variations of an 'I' configuration).

The knack of making tight joints

1 Tight joints rely on care and accuracy in initial marking out (see Measuring and Marking Out, page 38). First, your choice of marking instrument is vital, depending on the scale and nature of work. For precision cabinet work a marking knife makes the most accurate line. Hold it like a pen with forefinger pressing down. Draw the blade across at a shallow angle, close to the measuring tool, such as a try square. Ensure the square is squeezed firmly against the wood.

2 Clearly shade waste areas (those to be cut away). The most effective is diagonal shading because it is visibly arresting, and it is done with a medium/soft leaded pencil.

3 Many woodworkers use a pencil for marking out. Ideally a hard-leaded pencil gives the most accurate line but is difficult to see, whereas a soft-leaded one is bolder but blunts as it draws, which affects accuracy. A good example is when a line is 'squared' around the wood: where the lines meet up the two pencil thicknesses are apparent. An effective modern marking tool is a ballpoint pen, which leaves a bold and consistent line.

4 A tape measure is useful in woodworking generally but it must be remembered that it is not the most accurate method of measuring. The hook is loose and often graduations are inaccurate to 3mm (⅛in) over a 1m (3¼ft) length. You would not use a tape measure to mark out these tiny and precise joints (a dovetail variation designed by the author).

5 A steel rule gives the best accuracy and in fine woodworking you need to be able to measure in half millimetres (approximately ¹⁄₆₄in). Mark with a marking knife rather than a pencil as the latter will not be precise enough.

6 A tight joint relies on the springiness or 'give' of the wood, so you obviously need to make the joint slightly tight, but by how much is hard to quantify, especially as the variable factors are the size of the joint and the character and hardness of the wood. However a guide is that in a medium-density hardwood the joint might be about half a millimetre (approximately ¹⁄₆₄in) oversize. A tiny bevel or 'leading edge' helps ease the joint together.

7 A crucial factor is where on the line to make the saw cut. This is where the 'half millimetre' (approximately ¹⁄₆₄in) rule makes sense because you do not actually measure it, but instead you place the saw on the line, or just off it, so that the line remains after sawing. The line therefore serves as a cutting reference point.

8 This rule applies to lines marked and cut down the grain in which the springiness of the wood is a factor, but for lines marked across the grain, such as shoulder lines on joints, the cutaway portion is usually made right on the line. This is generally why shoulder lines are marked with a marking knife.

9 The final chisel cut is made by placing the tip of the chisel exactly on the line and very carefully removing the last portion of waste (see Dovetail Joints, page 94). Successful joint cutting (indeed all woodworking) also relies on the way you stand and hold tools.

10 When using a tenon saw, far greater control can be achieved by using both hands. There is twice the power and both elbows act as pivots, forcing correct alignment of the body, and in particular the eye, with the line to be cut (see Sawing, page 44).

▲ ALAN PETERS
TABLE
This low table is made of solid Andaman padauk with contrasting sycamore uprights, and it uses that most distinguishable of woodworking joints, the dovetail. Here, however, the joint in the top is echoed in the section of the vertical members. Because the direction of the grain is similar in all the components, the table will move freely as the ambient humidity changes. A subtle shoulder has been incorporated into the vertical rails to give strength to the top.

A totally mechanical joint
This is an ingenious Japanese joint called a 'Kanawa-tsugi' or mortised rabbeted oblique scarf joint. It is a challenge for any woodworker to make (this one is by the author) as it is an exercise in marking out and cutting. The intricate overlapping cutaway portions are tightly interlocked by a slightly tapered wedge, driving the two pieces together. When withdrawn the two pieces come apart. No glue is used and therefore this is a totally mechanical joint offering maximum strength. It also emphasises the visual honesty of joints – the structure is the aesthetic.

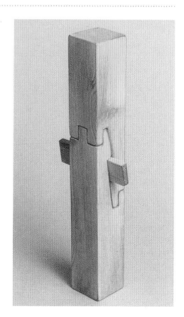

Butt and Lap Joints

The butt joint is the simplest of corner joints (if it can be called a joint at all) as it consists of two square-ended pieces of wood meeting together without any overlap. Because of this, it needs reinforcement by gluing, nailing or screwing. Glue alone will hold the joint together. However, it is not a very strong or permanent bond as the end grain absorbs much of the glue and end grain gluing should generally be avoided in woodworking. Subsequent timber movement (shrinkage) can cause the joint to come adrift over a period of time. A better reinforcement to the butt joint is to dowel it together (see Dowel Joints, page 80).

The lap joint, which is a development of the butt joint, combines a butt on one piece and a stepped cutout on the other. This gives slightly more mechanical integrity and a longer glue line for greater strength.

It also needs reinforcing with pins, which helps to hold the wood together while gluing (see Gluing, page 66). Butt and lap joints are used for lightweight frames and carcases of a joinery nature and for small boxes where the top and base pieces add to the strength of the joint.

However, despite the simplicity of butt and lap joints you will find they can be tricky to make. In fact when using hand tools, butt and lap joints involve one of the most difficult woodworking tasks – cutting the ends of the pieces of wood perfectly 'square' (90 degrees) (see Squaring Wood, page 54).

This is made much easier by the use of an appropriate power tool such as a circular saw, a radial-arm saw or a bandsaw, finishing off to a line with a disc sander.

Making a lap joint using hand tools
1 First prepare both pieces of timber to size (see Squaring Wood, page 54), paying particular attention to squaring off the ends of both pieces of wood. It is good practice to use a plane with a scrapwood block at the back of the work to prevent the timber from splitting. Work to a cut line and check the result with a try square.

CHECKLIST
- **Marking gauge**
- **Steel rule**
- **PVA glue**
- **Pins, nails or screws**
- **Tenon saw**
- **Pencil**
- **12mm (½in) chisel**
- **Mallet**
- **Smoothing or jack plane**
- **Table disc sander and power drill**
- **Radial-arm saw or small circular saw or small router**
- **Health and safety (pages 8–9)**

SOME COMMON USES OF BUTT AND LAP JOINTS

If additional strength is required, butt and laps can either be screwed or nailed together into the end grain.

Butt and lap joints can be used for right-angle or 'T' connections in areas where no great strength is required in the joint.

Butt and lap joints are used in both carcases and frameworks. Further strength is gained when a panel is added, as in the case of a basic box (carcase) and shallow tray (frame).

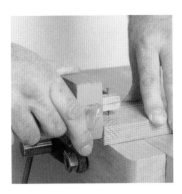

2 Set a marking gauge to the thickness of the wood and gauge a line on the face of the lapping piece. Then extend the lines on the edges to about two-thirds the thickness of the wood and reset the gauge to mark a narrow line along the end of the piece, extending it along the edges to meet up with the first line.

3 With a pencil, shade in the waste to be cut away. This clearly shows which portion of the wood is to be removed. Place the wood in the vice and use a tenon saw to cut down the grain, always working on the waste side of the line (see Sawing, page 44).

4 If you now place the wood in the vice at a slight angle, you can either saw across the grain to the line or remove the portion of waste with a chisel by cutting either with the grain or across it (see Chiselling, page 56).

5 Assuming the lap joint is part of a framework or small carcase, apply glue to the joints and assemble, using either pins, clamps or masking tape to pull the joints together.

Making a lap joint using power tools

1 Power tools are a much faster method of making lap joints. After squaring the timber, place two marks on the end of the piece to show the depth and width you will work to using a radial-arm saw. Pull the saw back to make a series of cuts. For multiple joint cutting a batten can be fixed for instant location of the workpiece. This can save you a lot of time.

2 Another quick method you might like to try is to clamp the piece to the bench and use the router (see page 60). Set this up with a straight cutter and fence to rout out the stepped portion.

Mitre Joints

A mitre joint comprises two pieces with their ends cut at 45 degrees that meet to form a right angle. A typical example is the corner of a picture frame, but the joint can also apply to the corner of a carcase.

On its own the mitre joint has no strength because the mating surfaces don't interlock; they simply butt against each other. For this reason it is usually glued with some kind of reinforcement, such as an internal tongue (see Biscuit and Domino Joints, page 82) or pins, dowels or veneer inserts. Because there is no visible end grain the joint offers some advantages; it is both visually pleasing and particularly suitable in constructions in which grooves can be later cut straight through to align in adjacent boards, or for continuous edge profiles.

The glue area of a mitre joint is curiously neither end grain nor side grain (see Jointing Principles, page 70) but tends to follow the characteristics of end grain, absorbing the glue and not forming a very strong bond.

On large-sectioned mitre joints the glue line tends to open up after a period of time, no matter how accurately the joint has been made. This is due to shrinkage or expansion.

The mitre joint can be cut with a handsaw, by various powered saws and also by purpose-built guillotines.

CHECKLIST
- **Mitre square or combination square**
- **Try square**
- **Steel rule**
- **Masking tape or 'G' clamps**
- **Hot-melt glue gun**
- **Tenon saw, dovetail saw or gentleman's saw**
- **Smoothing plane**
- **Circular sawbench**
- **Health and safety (pages 8–9)**

VARIOUS MITRE USES

Mitre joints are used for frames and carcases and are usually reinforced to stop them from breaking.

A typical way of reinforcing a mitre is with dowels. In this case accurate alignment is extremely important.

The mitre is ideal for shaped edges or grooves to be run continuously from one part of the joint to another.

Making a mitre joint by hand
1 Prepare the wood to size (see Squaring Wood, page 54). Use a mitre square to mark the 45 degree angles on both pieces. Extend the vertical lines using a try square. It is not always necessary to mark the line all the way around the wood, especially on thin-sectioned wood.

2 Place the wood on a bench-hook or clamp it to the bench using a 'G' clamp with the end extending over the benchtop. Use a tenon saw to cut to the line (see Sawing, page 44). Repeat the operation on the other piece, taking care to saw on the waste side of the line and checking the saw cut is vertical. Check the joint aligns perfectly, using a try square, and trim with a handplane if necessary. Keep to the marked line as this is the only accurate guide.

3 One way of gluing the mitre joint together is to use masking tape to stretch across the glue line. You first stretch a piece of tape across the centre, then add more strips and repeat the process, carefully turning the wood over to the other side to equalise the pressure. Masking tape is an improvised yet underrated woodworking aid.

4 Alternatively two 45 degree blocks can be fixed with a hot-melt glue gun to serve as temporary clamping blocks and chiselled off afterwards. It is important to line up the clamp with the centre of the glue line to obtain even pressure.

Making a framework mitre joint using a circular saw

1 Set up the circular saw so that the blade height clears above the thickness of the timber to be cut. Set the sliding mitre fence 'manually' by using a parallel piece of wood carefully set between saw teeth (note arrow marks) and a mitre square. Never rely on the calibrations of the machine, as this allows too much room for error.

2 Having prepared the wood to the required size, lower the saw blade guard into position, place the wood against the mitre fence to overlap the line of the saw blade, grip the wood firmly against the mitre fence and pass it slowly across the saw blade, keeping fingers well away from the blade. (Machine guard has been taken off for clarity of illustration.)

3 The other piece is sawn in the same way to make up the mitre joint. The circular saw can also be used with its parallel fence set so that a reinforced 'loose tongue' (see Edge Joints, page 78) can be grooved along the mitred ends of the wood. Lower the saw blade and test the method on a scrap piece first (see Sawing, page 44).

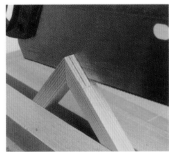

Making a veneer reinforced 'picture frame' mitre joint

1 This method is suitable for small-sectioned wood frames. Make the mitre joint by hand- or power-tool methods and glue it together. When dry, mount the joint in the vice and use a mitre square and pencil to mark a diagonal line to indicate the base line of the sawn veneer inserts. Then use a marking gauge to mark two lines dividing the thickness into thirds.

2 On a scrap piece of wood try out a saw cut using a tenon saw, dovetail saw or gentleman's saw to match the thickness of the cut to a selected piece of stout veneer (beech or ash). When you have established a suitable saw kerf (see Sawing, page 44), carefully cut down the marked lines on the wood.

3 Now insert the veneer into the saw cuts, trace around it and, using a marking knife and steel rule, carefully cut the veneer slightly oversize, ready for gluing.

4 Glue the veneer inserts into the saw cuts using PVA glue, spreading it liberally over all surfaces. Carefully slide the veneers into the saw cuts and leave to dry for at least 2 hours. Finally clean up the joint using a smoothing plane and/or abrasive block.

Edge Joints

When wide boards or panels are required, it is usually necessary to join together narrower pieces along their edges to make up the width. Timber boards vary in width, according to the species of tree from which they are cut. It is very rare for a tabletop, for instance, to be made from a single board.

The problem does not exist when using manufactured boards such as plywood, MDF or chipboard because they are available in larger sizes, such as 2440 × 1220mm (8 × 4ft), and by their composition they also avoid the problem of warping or otherwise twisting out of shape.

If you look at the end grain of any solid board you will notice the annual rings (more pronounced on some timbers than others). A rule of thumb is that the annual rings will try to straighten out when the timber dries out. This gives you an indication of which way the board will warp. If the annual rings are long, it means the board has been 'slice cut' from

the tree and is likely to warp more than a board with short annual rings (which is 'quarter' or 'radial' cut).

There are various methods of edge jointing. The simplest method is to butt joint the boards and glue and clamp them (see Gluing, page 66). For a stronger and more long-lasting bond the butt joint can be reinforced with dowel joints, biscuit joints or by using a long loose plywood tongue that slots into both faces of the joint. By using a special cutter in a router you can also make a 'tongue and groove' joint or a finger joint. These methods improve the mechanical strength and also lengthen the glue line across the section of the wood.

Edge jointing a small panel
1 Prepare some 100 × 18mm (4 × ¾in) boards to size (see Squaring Wood, page 54). Select the boards for visual interest (varying the grain and colour) and arrange them in a 'herringbone' fashion to minimise timber movement. Number the boards, as you will need this for future reference when assembling them.

2 Check that the edges of the boards are perfectly 'square' and straight. If you have planed the wood by machine, it is easier to achieve accuracy. It is important that the boards fit well and you should not rely on excessive clamping pressure to pull them in. If you take your time, it is not too difficult to get right.

CHECKLIST
- **Steel rule and try square**
- **6mm (¼in) straight bit**
- **6mm (¼in) birch plywood**
- **2–4 sash cramps**
- **PVA or synthetic resin glue**
- **Water bowl and cloth**
- **Handplane**
- **Planer-thicknesser**
- **Biscuit jointer or power drill, dowel jig and dowels, or router**
- **Health and safety (pages 8–9)**

HOW TO PREVENT WARPING WHEN EDGE JOINTING

slice cut

radial cut (or quarter sawn)

Timber is sawn from the log by 'slice' or 'radial' cut.

Wood that has been quarter or radial cut remains relatively stable on drying; slice-cut wood tends to warp as the rings have a tendency to straighten out when dry.

If you are using slice-cut timber it is best to alternate the rings into a herringbone configuration to help avoid bowing.

Large areas can be panelled with tongue-and-grooved board, as shrinkage is taken up in the joint.

For extra strength, instead of using a rubbed joint (as in the herringbone arrangement above), a finger joint can be made using a special router cutter.

3 Check that the board edges are perfectly flat with a steel rule or straight-edge.

4 You can edge joint the boards by a variety of methods, including a simple butt joint, dowel joint, biscuit joint or loose tongues.

5 Biscuit jointing is a quick and effective method for edge jointing and relies on a series of marks on the edge for the centre of the biscuit.

6 After edge jointing the boards, clamp them together to check that everything pulls up accurately. This is called a 'dry run' (see Gluing, page 66).

7 Apply glue to the joint surfaces and the inserts and place the whole assembly in clamps. For longer panels you will need to use perhaps three or four sash cramps, placing some on top to avoid bowing.

8 After checking that all the boards are flush (flat and level), persuading them with hammer and scrapwood if necessary, wipe away the excess glue with a damp cloth. This is very important and saves unnecessary work afterwards.

9 Leave the boards in the clamps (at least 2 hours for PVA and 8 hours for synthetic resin glue), then remove the panel and clean up the surfaces with a finely adjusted handplane. Working diagonally gives the most efficient cut (see Planing, page 48).

10 Alternatively you can use a finely set powered handplaner and gently skate over the surface.

Dowel Joints

The dowel joint is quick and simple to make because it consists of using small wooden pegs instead of hand-cut timber. It offers a versatile and strong system of wood connection requiring limited equipment. The joint can form any configuration of pieces, such as 'L' shaped, 'T' shaped or 'X' shaped etc, and it is often used instead of the mortise and tenon. To ensure the joint is strong, several dowels are used instead of the single tenon.

The joint comprises two pieces butt or mitred together (see Butt and Lap Joints, page 74) with a series of carefully aligned drill holes to accommodate the wood dowel. Normally the dowel is made of a stout wood, such as beech or ash, manufactured in short lengths of three main diameters, 6, 8 and l0mm (¼, ⁵⁄₁₆ and ⅜in), with flutings or grooves to allow the glue to disperse evenly. Without these the dowel can act as a piston and compress the glue in the hole. The quickest and most accurate method of dowel jointing is to use proprietary dowel centre points or a locating/drilling jig, both of which are readily available from good tool shops (see also Jointing Principles, page 70).

CHECKLIST
- **Steel rule and marking gauge**
- **Dowel rods**
- **Appropriate size dowel drilling bit**
- **Drill depth-stop collar**
- **Dowel jig or dowel centres or panel pins and pliers**
- **PVA glue**
- **Clamps**
- **Electric power drill**
- **Health and safety (pages 8–9)**

MULTI-DOWEL JOINT
Using several dowels instead of one is the modern equivalent of the mortise and tenon joint. Small brass centring points help to secure the joint.

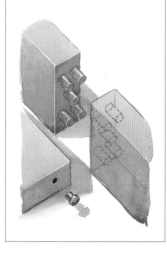

Making a dowel joint with dowel centre points
1 After the timber has been accurately prepared to size (see Squaring Wood, page 54), mark out the centre lines on the end of the wood using a try square, steel rule and marking gauge.

2 Select the appropriate diameter dowel centre point and, with the same diameter drill bit, drill the holes. You should position yourself in line with the wood so that you can guide the drill parallel to the sides of the timber. To ensure you do not drill in too far, use tape or a proprietary depth-stop attached to the drill bit.

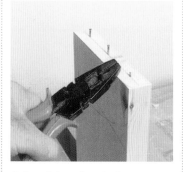

A dowel-locating device
A simple alternative to dowel centre points is to use a panel pin as a dowel-locating device. Drive the pin in and take off the head with a pair of cutters or pliers. Locate the matching hole and after the pieces have been pressed together, withdraw the pin with the cutters or pliers.

Using a dowelling jig
1 Mark the positions of the dowel joints by squaring a line across the wood. No matter how good the tool you are using is, the initial marking out is critical. The golden rule in all woodwork is measure twice and cut once. Clamp the dowel jig to the bench and clamp the wood with the marked line visible in the centre of the jig drilling hole.

3 It is important to use a special dowel bit that has a centre point so as to locate the marked position accurately. Twist drills are liable to wander. Flat bits can sometimes be used but they have a long centre point that is not suitable for drilling into thin boards.

4 For marking off the positions on the corresponding piece, insert the proprietary dowel centre barrels into the holes.

5 Use the pointed end to mark off the corresponding drill hole positions. For a 'T'-configuration joint you can square a guide line across the wood, with which the edge of the first piece can align. Then either press or drive the pieces together.

6 Drill out the corresponding holes, taking care to drill straight and square; this can be tricky, so be careful. Apply glue to the dowel rod, the dowel holes and the edge of the boards, and clamp the work together (see Gluing, page 66).

2 Using the appropriate dowel bit and with the depth-stop attached, carefully drill through the guide hole in the jig, straight into the wood. Move the wood along to drill subsequent holes in the same manner.

3 Now insert the other piece of wood into the jig, using the clamps in the adjacent position. Align the marked positions with the jig drilling hole.

4 Drill out the holes in turn. The jig clamps will need to be rearranged to drill all the holes.

5 The dowel joint should align perfectly, ready for gluing (see page 66).

Biscuit and Domino Joints

Although they look similar and are used in essentially the same way, biscuit and domino jointers have slightly different functions. The biscuit jointer is primarily an edge-jointing tool, with the joint requiring additional support through the design. The domino provides a more robust jointing system and can be used in a wider range of applications, but is more expensive.

Biscuit jointing

The biscuit joint combines a simple butt or mitre joint with an elliptical compressed wood insert called a biscuit that gives the joint its strength. The biscuit housing is easily located and cut by the biscuit jointer – a small-diameter circular saw with a plunging cutter. The tool comprises a spring-loaded cutter assembly/motor housing, a baseplate and adjustable guide fence with an additional bevel fence for inserting biscuits into mitre joints. You can adjust the depth of cut to suit the biscuit, and the blade can also be finely adjusted horizontally.

The biscuit itself is made of compressed beech and is available in three sizes. The entire joint is glued, usually with PVA glue, which causes the biscuit to swell. For multiple biscuit joints, a slower-working glue should be used such as a synthetic glue.

Biscuit joints can never be as strong as traditional joints, such as the mortise and tenon or dovetail, but they are ideal for constructions such as small boxes, kitchen cupboards and edge jointing solid wood boards in which the joint serves as a locating system for keeping adjoining boards flush when gluing. In thicker frameworks the biscuits can be double inserted across the thickness of the stock, but the joint should be used for centre rails and not as a replacement for a mortise and tenon on corners of frameworks.

Domino jointing

The domino jointer has an oscillating milling cutter instead of a moving saw blade. It is used in the same manner as the biscuit jointer to cut slots into which wooden splines, called dominoes, can be fitted. The resulting joint is robust and is especially useful as a substitute for mortise and tenon joints.

By changing the size of the cutter and adjusting the depth stop, slots can be cut to fit different-sized dominoes, which come in various lengths and thicknesses. The jointer also has a fence that can be tilted for mitre cuts or moved vertically to adjust the distance of the domino from the top surface.

CHECKLIST
- **Ballpoint pen/pencil**
- **Rule**
- **Biscuit jointer or domino jointer**
- **Hammer**
- **Sash cramps**
- **'G' clamps**
- **PVA or synthetic glue**
- **Health and safety (pages 8–9)**

Biscuit jointing

1 Prepare the ends of panels for jointing (butt joint), ensuring the joint surfaces are true and flat. You can hand plane them or use them straight off the machine saw but they must be accurate.

Mark out the biscuit joint centres on the panels to be jointed, copying one from the other. For a 'T' configuration, a squared line across the panel will help to position the adjacent member.

SOME APPLICATIONS FOR BISCUIT JOINTS

Biscuit joints are a versatile modern system that can be used to form joints in a variety of simple butt configurations.

Biscuit joints can be used to edge joint narrow boards for use in making up tabletops or other wide surfaces.

A biscuit jointer can be used to join together the sides of a drawer and also to groove out for the base.

Double biscuit joints can be used on sturdy sections such as centre rails where the load is not too excessive.

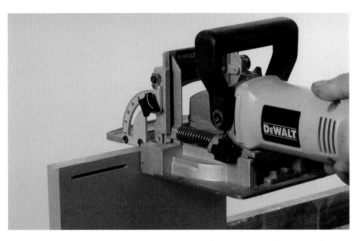

2 Now clamp the panel to the bench and set the tool for cutter depth, adjusting the fence so that the biscuit is central across the thickness of the panel. Align the tool with the marked position on the panel and carefully make a plunge cut. Then withdraw without disturbing the position. Repeat the action for multiple joints.

3 When cutting slots in the adjoining panel for an 'L' joint, secure the panel upright in a vice. Align the cutter and fence and

carefully make a plunge cut for the corresponding joint. Take your time doing this and work slowly and deliberately.

4 For a 'T' joint, turn the jointer around so that it is standing vertically. Align the jointer along the squared pencil line, positioning it to the biscuit centre mark. You can 'G' clamp a batten on the panel and butt the flat face of the jointer against this to use as a guide. Carefully plunge the tool to make the matching cut.

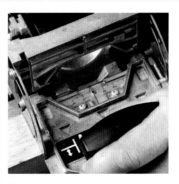

5 For maximum strength mitre cuts, the fence has to be set so that the biscuit centre is slightly nearer the inner face of the panel. Some biscuit jointers have a separate mitre fence, or you could make one from an angled block of scrapwood. Secure the panel and carefully plunge the tool at the marked positions.

6 Glue biscuit joints together with PVA glue, using a thin wood spatula to coat every surface. Remember that chipboard absorbs glue, so be generous and work quickly. Drive the joint home with a hammer and scrapwood block, using sash cramps (see Gluing, page 66). If there is a lot of gluing to be done, then instead of PVA use a synthetic glue, which takes longer to set.

Domino jointing
1 Using the same procedure as for biscuit jointing, mark the domino positions on the wood and then mortise into the wood at the marked positions. As the domino jointer can cut deeper than the biscuit jointer, be more careful about checking the depth of cut to ensure that you do not go all the way through the piece.

2 Fit the dominoes and assemble the joint. Dominoes are a very snug fit into the standard slots, so it is useful to make a set of dominoes that have been thinned slightly for use in dry runs. You can create these by sanding or taking off a couple of shavings with a block plane. Stain the dry-run dominoes with a bright colour, so that they don't get mixed up with the standard ones.

Halving Joints

Strong, attractive and quick, to make, the halving joint has many applications. It is one of woodworking's strongest wood joints because equal portions are removed from each member and optimum fibre overlap ensures the strongest leverage in one direction. Therefore one member is not weakened any more than the other because in all halving joints both members are always the same geometry. As there is no mechanical binding of the joint, a strong glue bond is required for the inner overlapping surfaces.

However, until fairly recently the joint relied on nails or screws as well as glue to hold it together. The advent of modern 'permanent' glues has now made it a truly versatile joint for 'L', 'T' and 'X' configurations in frameworks and some modern 'permanent' glues are quite sufficient to hold it in both indoor and outdoor applications, without any further assistance.

The basic technique for cutting all the configurations of this joint are the same but it is useful here to look at hand cutting the 'X' configuration because, of the three, it is both the strongest and most commonly used.

CHECKLIST
- **Pencil or ballpoint pen**
- **Marking gauge**
- **Try square**
- **Tenon saw**
- **Chisel**
- **Mallet**
- **Hammer and scrapwood**
- **Radial-arm saw**
- **'G' clamp and batten**
- **Health and safety (pages 8–9)**

Cutting an 'L' halving joint on the radial-arm saw

This example is for the 'L' configuration of the halving joint, but it could be used for any other. The radial-arm saw is predominantly for use in cutting across the grain, where, by taking a series of very closely spaced cuts across the grain of the joint, it eliminates the need to chisel down the grain for cleaning away the waste.

Tightly spaced cuts allow the remaining waste simply to be snapped off. In fact if the cuts made are sufficiently close together all the waste will be removed by the saw, and no cleaning up with a chisel will be necessary. Remember that with a saw of this type there will be considerable 'set' on the blade and this will result in a much wider 'kerf' or width-of-cut than you will get with a handsaw.

1 After you have marked the wood for width and depth of cut and adjusted the blade height (checking the cut is centred), draw the saw head across in a series of narrow cuts.

2 The narrow strips of 'short grain' are easily removed by knocking the wood against a benchtop, and then the surface is perfectly levelled using the radial-arm saw.

3 It should be possible to achieve a perfectly flush joint even if the contact surfaces have to be reworked fractionally on the radial-arm saw.

Cutting an 'X' halving joint by hand

1 After preparing the timber to size (see Squaring Wood, page 54), trace the width of each piece on the corresponding piece with a pencil or ballpoint pen.

2 Using a try square held with the stock against the face side of the timber, extend the marks both across the wood and to halfway down the edges.

3 With a marking gauge set to exactly half the thickness of the wood, gauge the depth lines using the stock of the gauge against the face side. Shade in the waste (see Measuring and Marking Out, page 38).

4 Fix the wood firmly in the vice and saw carefully on the waste side of the line with a tenon saw, to the halfway mark (see Sawing, page 44).

5 After sawing the other line, checking it carefully against the width of the other piece, chisel away the waste wood (see Chiselling, page 56). Work into the centre, then turn the wood around and repeat the action to avoid splitting the end fibres. A mallet greatly helps to control the chiselling action. The chiselling is done in 2–3mm (approximately ⅛in) cuts at a time. Make finer chisel cuts as you approach the line.

6 Now check for flatness with the edge of the chisel. Repeat the process on the other piece of wood, checking the position of the sawn lines, which are crucial for a tight fit.

An alternative chisel method is to make tapered cuts from each direction to form a 'hilltop', then chisel horizontally back to the line.

7 Carefully chisel a slight 'leading edge' where the joint will fit together. This will prevent too much pressure from having to be applied and will gradually ease the two halves into position.

8 Squeeze the joint together by using a vice. If it is too tight, plane a fraction off the side edges in preference to chiselling back the saw line; chiselling is difficult to do accurately because the error is likely to be very fine and you would be chiselling across the grain in small bites. Then clean up the surfaces using a smoothing plane.

Housing Joints

The housing, or dado as it is often called, is a strong, simple joint whereby a groove is cut across the grain of one piece of wood into which another piece is fitted. The joint is usually found in cabinet construction for shelves and dividers in furniture such as dressers or bookcases.

In its simplest form, the housing joint consists of a shallow-bottomed groove running the full width of the timber into which the square-edged piece sits. Variations of the joint include stopped shoulders – where the groove does not run the full width of the timber, so the joint is not visible from the front – and dovetail-sectioned grooves for maximum mechanical strength, which are nowadays most often cut with a router.

Housings that go along the grain rather than across it, such as in drawer making, are similar in construction but tend to be much narrower owing to the thinness of material used in drawer bottoms.

The joint is normally glued and in crude constructions pins or screws can be used to reinforce it; the groove prevents the pin or screw from splitting narrow-section timber and gives the joint added grip.

There are various ways to make housing or dado joints by hand, power tool or machine, such as using jigged tool-guiding blocks (see Jigs and Jigmaking, page 63), or with saws and chisels or by fast cutting with a radial-arm saw

(see Sawing, page 44). You will find that power tools are much quicker and usually more accurate but hand skills are well worth developing for your own satisfaction as a craftsperson.

CHECKLIST
- **Marking knife or pencil**
- **Try square**
- **Steel rule or straight-edge**
- **Marking gauge**
- **Two 'G' clamps**
- **Batten**
- **Tenon saw**
- **Paring chisel and/or router plane**
- **Small electric router**
- **Straight fence**
- **Straight cutter**
- **Dovetail cutter**
- **Health and safety (pages 8–9)**

Making a through housing joint by hand
1 Prepare the wood accurately to size (see Squaring Wood, page 54). Mark out the position of the joint on the piece to be grooved by tracing thickness marks on to it using a marking knife, pencil or ballpoint pen.

2 Extend the lines across the wood using a large try square or by extending the reach of a standard one by placing a straight-edge next to it (see Measuring and Marking Out, page 38).

6 Remove the waste with a chisel and mallet. The fibres should break away quite easily as they are weak across the grain where they have been severed lengthways by the saw.

7 By using the bevel of the chisel tip you can cut in further without the handle fouling the wood, but this takes a little more skill. This is because there is less of the tool in contact with the wood and this makes it harder to control.

3 Now extend lines to about one-third of the thickness of the wood with the try square on the other face, to give you the depth of the groove to be cut (this one-third is a general rule). Set a marking gauge and mark the line on both ends of the piece. Shade in the waste to show clearly which part has to be removed.

4 Secure the workpiece to the bench with one or two 'G' clamps and use a tenon saw to cut the walls of the housing joint to the line. For extra control you can use both hands on the saw handle. Try it each way and see which suits you best.

5 The saw should cut just on the waste side of the line, leaving the thickness of the line intact. This will give you a nice snug fit (see Jointing Principles, page 70).

8 Now turn the wood around and chisel in from the other side (see Chiselling, page 56), working down to the bottom of the housing in a series of fine cuts.

9 Alternatively you can use a router plane with its adjustable hooked cutter. Set it to depth each time to make a series of 3mm (⅛in) cuts. The wood fibres break up easily.

10 The advantage of using a router plane is that it levels the bottom of the housing perfectly because the base of the plane sits on the surface of the wood either side of the groove, thus making it impossible to cut too deeply if the cutter is set to the correct depth. You may wish to combine the methods by first removing the bulk of the waste quickly with chisel and mallet.

11 Plane a fractional bevel on the end of the other piece to create a 'leading edge' for ease of entry and persuade the two pieces together using a hammer and piece of scrapwood to avoid any bruising. Make sure the ends are flush.

Making a dovetailed stopped housing or dado joint with an electric router

1 The dovetailed housing is cut in stages, using a straight cutter and then a dovetail cutter to prolong the life of both. This eases the path of the more bulky dovetail cutter and thus reduces its workload. It is impossible to lower the dovetail cutter in a series of shallow cuts because of its shape. It must always be introduced into the wood from the side.

First set up a plunging router with a small straight cutter. Then clamp a batten to the wood to serve as a guide. The router is placed on the wood, the cutter in line with the groove, and the batten is clamped tight against the side of the router. Mark with a pencil where the groove stops. Now rout a series of shallow stepped cuts down to almost full depth.

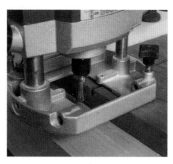

2 Replace the straight cutter with the appropriately sized dovetail cutter, setting the depth-stop so that the cutter achieves the full profiled cut in one pass. You can now see that because the bulk of the waste has been removed more gently with the straight cutter, the dovetail cutter can open up the desired profile.

3 Carefully rout out the dovetailed housing in one pass, being sure to keep the router pressed tight against the batten. Do not be tempted to release the plunge mechanism at the end of the cut but withdraw the cutter back along its own path. For wider-sectioned dovetailed housing place a packing strip next to the batten so that a second cut can be made next to the first.

4 You will find that the best way to fashion the dovetailed shoulders of the other piece is to set the router upside down in a router table, using the same cutter. Router tables are quite cheap to buy and you will find that they increase the scope of a router tremendously. Set the adjustments for depth and width of cut. The wood is passed through to cut one side and then the other.

5 Now remove the stopped portion by first sawing down the grain with a tenon or dovetail saw (see Sawing, page 44) and then across the grain. The stopped portion, remember, has to be cut away because in this case the groove on the other piece did not go right across the full width of the wood. For proper control, make sure the wood is firm in the vice and adjusted so that each sawing operation is executed vertically.

6 Because the end of the dovetailed housing is curved to follow the cutter shape, you have to round off the end of the joint to match. This is simply done with a sharp chisel.

7 Carefully slide the two pieces together ready for gluing. There is a tendency for wide panels to warp, making it difficult to withdraw 'dry' joints, so gluing should commence as soon as possible (see Gluing, page 66).

◄ BODDINGTON & FOOTE
LECTERN

The lectern, which is designed to bear weights of up to 10kg (22lb), is made of solid African wenge. It is laminated from sawn-cut veneers and glued together with epoxy resin in a male and female laminating mould. The laminates are joined together with housing joints and by a stainless steel core, which is threaded through and has T-nuts on the ends. The fixings are hidden in the counter bores and covered by turned wenge pellets. The floor laminates have a lead core, which lowers the centre of gravity. The piece is finished with a basecoat of acid-catalysed lacquer before being burnished and waxed with teak wax.

▼ EDWARD HOPKINS
NESTING TABLES

The simple but excellently executed design allows the quality of the materials to shine through. The bold frame-and-panel construction includes the use of large mortise and tenon joints, and the medullary ray of evergreen oak is especially eye-catching here. The superb construction allows each table to be slid smoothly out along its housing with just one hand.

Mortise and Tenon Joints

The mortise and tenon – easily identified by its 'tongue' and 'mouth' components – is probably the most common woodworking joint. Being widely used for doors and frames over the years, its place is firmly entrenched in history.

It was originally a 'dry' joint, often held together with wooden pegs before the advent of glues, and therefore is predominantly a mechanical joint – even when the glue breaks down, as it does in many old pieces, the joint still works (see Jointing Principles, page 70).

The mortise and tenon family

The mortise and tenon refers to a family of joints and the most basic one is the through mortise and tenon, which offers maximum strength as the 'tongue' extends to the full depth of the 'mouth'. The hidden 'stub tenon' joint penetrates to about two-thirds the width of the wood. It is these two particular joints that we look at in detail here, although there are very many variations.

Long- and short-shouldered mortise and tenons accommodate rebates on one face. Haunch mortise and tenons are used in corner frames of wide sections to avoid warping.

Bare-faced tenons have no shoulders and are therefore quicker to make but in general a shoulder all the way around offers better anchorage and conceals the tricky part of making, which is the fit of the tenon in the mortise.

The mortise and tenon can be cut by hand- or power-tool methods, particularly the tenon which in essence is a double-rebated member. As a framework corner joint ('L' configuration) the haunch mortise and tenon is a useful joint to make and varies in detail from the technique of making a through mortise and tenon for a 'T' configuration.

CHECKLIST
- **Marking knife, pencil or ballpoint pen**
- **Steel rule**
- **Try square**
- **Mortise gauge**
- **Tenon saw**
- **Hammer and scrapwood block**
- **Marking gauge**
- **6mm (¼in) mortise chisel**
- **Mallet**
- **12mm (½in) bevel-edged chisel**
- **Smoothing plane**
- **Powered mortiser**
- **12mm (½in) mortising bit**
- **Radial-arm saw with tungsten-carbide tipped (TCT) blade**
- **Health and safety (pages 8–9)**

Cutting a through mortise and tenon by hand
1 Prepare the wood to size (see Squaring Wood, page 54). Then mark out the shoulder lines on the tenon to correspond with the width of the wood. Leave 1mm (about ¹⁄₃₂in) for cleaning up afterwards. Then mark two lines across the mortise piece to correspond with the width of the tenon minus 1mm (about ¹⁄₃₂in) for cleaning up afterwards. Place code marks 'A' on the wood for clarity.

2 As the tenon goes all the way through the other piece, the mortise has to be marked on both edges, so extend the marks to the other edge using a try square with its stock held against the face on the waste side of the line down the tenon faces.

A BASIC MORTISE AND TENON AND A HAUNCHED VARIATION

The basic mortise and tenon is a simple joint where the square tenon (tongue) fits snugly into the mortise (mouth). This common joint has been used in furniture making for centuries in this, the most elementary, form.

A haunched mortise and tenon is a variation that involves the addition of an extra part designed to give strength if the joint is used on the corners of frames.

3 A double-spurred mortise gauge is used to mark the corresponding tenon and mortise width; usually this is about one-third of the thickness of the timber. In this case the timber is 18mm (¾in) thick and a 6mm (¼in) mortise chisel is used – they come in sizes of 6mm, 9mm and 12mm (¼, ⅜ and ½in). Set the spurs slightly wider than the chisel width.

4 Now set the stock of the gauge so that the spurs centralise across the thickness of the wood and gauge the lines using the stock against the face side. Gauge both edges.

5 Mount the tenon piece in the vice and carefully use the gauge with the same setting to correspond with the mortise. The marking out is now completed.

6 Mount the wood firmly on the bench in line with a leg. The best way to do this is to use a piece of scrapwood in the vice, then clamp the workpiece to it. Stand at the end of the bench in line with the mortise. Using the chisel and mallet, make a series of fine cuts at 3mm (⅛in) intervals from the centre towards each end. Use a try square to guide the alignment of the chisel.

7 A waste portion is needed for levering the chippings out, so do not chisel right up to the line. The depth of cut of the mallet stroke is about 6mm (¼in) each time, depending on the type of wood. In hardwoods you may have to take a little less than this. Now carefully lever the chippings out. Repeat this process in staged depths.

8 You can see how the chisel pivots on the waste area left when removing the chippings. After you have cut through to about halfway, reverse the timber and repeat the action.

9 When remounting the wood, take care to clear debris from the benchtop as it can dent the finished work.

10 Now stand in front of the bench and carefully chisel the mortise end walls vertically. A try square helps align the cut. It is important the ends are flat and square. As the mortise gauge was set slightly over the thickness of the chisel, a fractional amount is now left for paring with a wider chisel. This is to ensure the mortise side walls are perfectly flat and vertical.

11 To cut the tenon, shade the waste to clarify which portions should be cut away, then mount the tenon piece in the vice vertically and use a tenon saw to cut away the cheeks. Take care to cut on the waste side of the line, leaving the line intact (see Jointing Principles, page 70). Alternatively tilt the wood and cut diagonally so two lines can be followed at the same time, giving greater saw control.

12 Using either the vice or a bench-hook, now saw the tenon cheeks across the grain exactly to the shoulder line. Accuracy is required as this shows on the finished joint.

13 To remove the preparation marks, clean up both pieces with a very finely set plane. This is why the mortise width was marked at 1mm (about ⅟₃₂in) under the tenon width. Plane a slight bevel or 'leading edge' on the end of the tenon. This will ease its path when it comes to assembling the joint.

14 Carefully drive the joint home using a hammer and scrapwood. If it is too tight, take the joint apart and examine where it is binding and pare with a chisel; however you should always aim for a joint 'straight off the saw' rather than one you have to chisel back.

As the tenon was marked out 1mm (about ⅟₃₂in) oversize, carry out the final assembly of the joint in the vice. Plane the joint flush.

Using a radial-arm saw to cut a tenon
1 The tenon can be cut with a variety of power tools. Here the radial-arm saw is used to swiftly achieve the task. Set the blade height to the marks on the wood. (The guards have been removed for clarity of illustration.)

2 Clamp a batten to the saw table as a shoulder-line depth-stop. To remove the waste, hold the wood firmly against the fence and draw the saw head across in a series of cuts. Rotate the wood to cut the other shoulder.

3 Now lower the saw head to cut the tenon cheeks. Using the batten as a stop, draw the saw back in a series of cuts right up to the shoulder line. Take care on the final cuts as the shoulders must align all the way around the wood. Trim a slight bevel on the tip of the tenon.

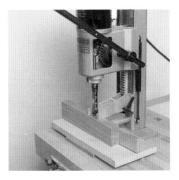

**Making a stub mortise
using the mortiser**
1 After preparing the wood to size, mark the position of the mortise on the wood. Select a chisel bit that corresponds to about one-third the thickness of the wood. Mark the depth of the mortise, which should extend to about two-thirds the width of the wood. Code the joints for clarity.

2 With a steel rule calculate the position of the tenon dimensions and make two marks.

3 Set a marking gauge and line in the marks accurately, adjusting the gauge by knocking it on the bench (see Measuring and Marking Out, page 38) and gauging from both sides.

4 Set up the mortiser with the appropriate bit and set the depth guide, using the timber marks for alignment. Adjust the fence so that the bit aligns perfectly to the gauged lines and position the top clamp so that the wood can slide comfortably underneath.

5 In a series of gentle cuts using the lever arm, chisel out the mortise, holding the wood firmly against the fence. Cut to the full depth in one pass.

6 Then slide the wood along so that the next cut overlaps the previous one. You may need to lift the bit clear for shavings to fully escape.

Fitting the joints
1 The finished mortise and tenon should have tight shoulder lines and be truly aligned as it is placed on the flat surface of the benchtop.

2 Now drive the joint together using a hammer and piece of scrapwood and finally clean up with a handplane.

Dovetail Joints

No other woodworking joint has the universal appeal of the dovetail. It seems to express the whole spirit of wood craftsmanship and yet, paradoxically, as a joint it is virtually redundant today in its strictest mechanical sense. There are other joints that, combined with the advantages of modern 'permanent' glues, are just as strong and a lot quicker to make.

Traditionally the dovetail was used by cabinet makers in the fronts of drawers; the pull of the drawer acted against the wedged design of the joint, making it very strong. This is because the greater the pull on the handle, the tighter the joint became. The effect was to pull the joint together rather than apart. The dovetail will probably always hold great appeal, not just visually but also as a challenge for woodworkers to make in its variety of forms. In hand woodworking it is commonly regarded as the last bastion of craftsmanship.

It can be made by hand or machine, and dovetail jigs involving the router (see Routing, page 60) now make the machine dovetail look as good as the hand-cut version. There are various types of dovetail, including lap dovetails, secret-mitred dovetails, single dovetails and common dovetails. All basically depend upon the same wedge shape to give them mechanical strength, so the common dovetail is shown here to illustrate the technique.

CHECKLIST
- **Try square**
- **Steel rule**
- **Marking knife**
- **Pencil**
- **Marking gauge**
- **Dovetail scriber**
- **Dovetail template or sliding bevel**
- **Dovetail saw**
- **Coping saw**
- **Bevel-edged chisel(s)**
- **Mallet**
- **Hammer and scrapwood**
- **Handplane**
- **Proprietary dovetail jig**
- **Router (ideally 1300 watts plus)**
- **Appropriate dovetail and straight cutters (tungsten-carbide tipped or high-speed steel)**
- **Health and safety (pages 8–9)**

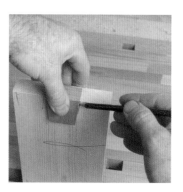

Marking out a common dovetail joint
1 After preparing the wood to size (see Squaring Wood, page 54), on each piece mark light shoulder lines all the way around to the thickness of the other piece plus 1mm (¹⁄₃₂in). You can use a try square and marking knife, keeping the stock against the face marks.

2 Using a dovetail template and pencil, mark out the positions of the dovetails on one piece. Always shade in the waste. The pitch angle is usually around 1:7 and can be marked alternatively with a sliding bevel. Pitch is the term used to denote the angle of the slope.

3 Using a try square, square the lines across the end of the wood and shade in the waste. This is very important so you know which bits to cut out.

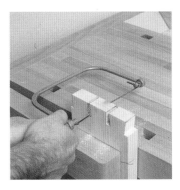

Sawing the joint

1 Secure the workpiece in the vice and tilt at an angle so that you can saw the dovetails vertically. You will find this aids accurate cutting because gravity naturally pushes the saw downwards. Use a dovetail saw for fine work. It is crucial to saw on the waste side of the line, leaving the entire line intact.

2 Using a try square and marking knife, deepen the shoulder line where the joint is to be cut.

3 Remove the end waste with a tenon saw, working down across the grain, carefully to the line.

4 Remove the waste with a coping saw, cutting to about 3mm (⅛in) of the shoulder line. The 3mm (⅛in) is left on at this stage because it can only be removed accurately with a very sharp chisel.

Chiselling the joint

1 Chisel back to the shoulder line using a bevel-edged chisel and mallet; use a series of fine vertical cuts to half the thickness of the wood. Then turn the wood around to cut from the other side. This will prevent the wood fibres from splitting or breaking out.

2 Finally clean up the shoulder lines with the chisel by mounting the wood back in the vice.

Transferring the marks

1 Now mount the second piece of wood in the vice at the raised level of a spacer piece, laid on the benchtop to ensure it lies flat, and carefully place the first piece (with tails cut) on to it. Align the shoulder lines and far edges perfectly. Trace the joint using a sharp pencil or dovetail scriber. Then shade in the waste.

2 Extend the vertical lines down the front of the joint using a try square. Now shade the waste wood using a series of clear diagonal lines. It makes cutting much easier.

Cutting the matching piece
1 Carefully use a dovetail saw to cut on the waste side of the line down the grain to the shoulder line.

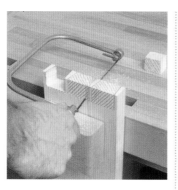

2 As before, a coping saw is used to remove the waste nearly to the line. Be careful not to cut into the angled pins.

Chiselling the matching piece
1 You can deepen the cut on the shoulder line to define it clearly for chiselling back.

2 Carefully chisel back to the shoulder line, overlapping each chisel cut to maintain a straight line. A narrow chisel gives much better control (see Chiselling, page 56).

Clamping up
1 Clamp the dovetail joint together using a cutout scrap block to allow the fingers to squeeze together up to the shoulder line. Using the scrap block prevents bruising from the clamp and also helps to spread the pressure from the clamp more evenly. Check the joint is square with a try square (see Gluing, page 66).

2 After gluing, clean up the joint with a plane, working inwards to avoid splitting the end grain on the joint itself. The edges of the joint can be planed diagonally to tidy them up, holding the wood in the vice.

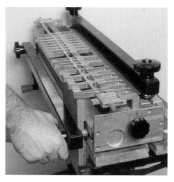

Using a jig to make a common dovetail joint
1 A particular jig was used in this demonstration – some features it shares with other jigs; other features are unique. If you do use a jig, first read the manufacturer's manual thoroughly to familiarise yourself with the particular type. Having read the manufacturer's manual, set up the jig and insert the wood for cutting the tails.

2 The positions of dovetails can be quickly set by tightening up the adjustable reversible fingers using the template in the 'pins' mode.

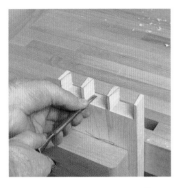

3 Now place the wood in the vice so that you can chisel horizontally to clean up the shoulder line. Take care not to cut right across, otherwise you will split the fibres.

4 Use a chisel to pare a fine bevel on the inside of the dovetails as a leading edge for pressing the joint together. This will ease the assembly of the joint.

Assembly and gluing
1 Carefully drive the joint home either by squeezing it in the vice or using a hammer and piece of scrapwood.

2 If everything fits well together, take the joint apart and coat the mating surfaces with glue using a fine spatula.

3 Reverse the template to the 'tails' mode and lock into position with the tightening screws. Then set up the router (see page 60) with the appropriate dovetail cutter and guide bush (refer to the manufacturer's manual). Mark the thickness of the other piece of wood to indicate the shoulder line of the joint, and set the depth of cut accordingly on the router.

4 Carefully rout the waste away to form the dovetails. A little practice is needed to avoid grain tear as the cutter comes out of the wood. Masking tape can help prevent fibres from splitting.

5 Remove the tails piece and insert the pins piece in the jig, marking the shoulder line as before.
    Reverse the jig template and position according to the appropriate guide marks on the jig. Insert the appropriate straight cutter in the router and set to depth. First make a series of shallow cuts across the width of the pins.

6 You can see by the profile of the jig fingers how the dovetail cutter and the straight cutter are used on their respective pieces. Here the straight cutter removes the waste for the pins in a series of fine cuts. After a little practice the jig can be fine-tuned to such a degree that finished dovetails will squeeze together by hand without any gaps showing. Glue and clamp as for the hand-cut dovetail.

Bending Wood

A natural characteristic of wood is that it bends. Some woods, however, are more bendy than others. Ash, beech and yew, for example, yield more easily than mahogany or teak. This section looks at ways in which you can bend wood, which will open up enormous creative possibilities.

A thin-cut section of wood bends more easily than a stout section, and when it is wet or hot it is even more pliable. Bending is an economic way to fashion the material because forming curves by jointing straight pieces and then shaping them (see Shaping Wood, page 101) is more complex, time-consuming and wasteful in material.

The main wood bending techniques are: steam bending, laminating and saw kerfing (although saw kerfing offers very little strength because most of the fibres are cut through). It is also possible to bend wood using microwave technology and this can be easily done with a domestic microwave although, because of the restriction of size, the method is most suited to modelmaking or shaping inlay strips (see Veneering, page 114).

There is no doubt that bends or curves in furniture are pleasing to the eye and with a little imagination and improvisation you can make up your own bending jigs. You can apply the method to all sorts of domestic items from salad servers and clock cases to chair backs or even complete chairs.

Saw kerfing

Saw kerfing is the least strong of all the bending methods. In fact because the wood is all but cut through its entire thickness, it offers very little strength and would only be suitable for non-load bearing applications such as plinths with curved corners.

Sometimes two saw kerfed bends can be glued together with the saw cuts facing innermost but, generally, care has to be taken not to split the fibres when bending away from the saw cuts.

The method can be achieved with a handsaw and jig or with a bandsaw against a stop, and the most quick and efficient method is with a radial-arm saw.

Laminating

Numerous thin strips or laminations of wood – up to 3mm (⅛in) thick – are cut and then glued together and bent around a former, usually a male and female mould. The terms male and female when applied to moulds refer to convex and concave shapes that usually match.

The grain follows the length of the strips and the use of a synthetic glue makes a very strong bond.

The method is suited to mass production as the machining and gluing is automated. Highly precise stainless-steel hydraulically operated moulds are used in conjunction with rapid microwave glue curing.

Low-cost individual laminating can be achieved by sawing thin strips and forming them in a chipboard male and female former. However, sawing does produce some wastage as the saw kerf can almost be as thick as the laminate. It is important to leave the glue to cure overnight before taking the wood out of the former.

Steam bending

Steam bending involves putting the timber in a sealed chamber that is filled with steam from a constant source; on a small scale this can even be a domestic kettle. When it is fully saturated the timber is taken out and bent with force around a shaped former.

The method is somewhat 'hit and miss' as the final bend may straighten out slightly when dry, and bends that are too tight can break. It is rare for wood thicker than about 35mm (1⅜in) to be steam bent, although 50mm (2in) has been achieved in some industrial production such as the seats of the classic Thonet chairs. Even then, a percentage of the tight bends break in the process.

Steam bending is particularly suited to home workshop low-cost improvisation.

CHECKLIST
- **Health and safety (pages 8–9)**

SAW KERFING
- **Pencil or ballpoint pen**
- **'G' clamps and/or sash cramps**
- **Handsaw or bandsaw**
- **Jig**
- **Radial-arm saw**

LAMINATING
- **Chipboard or MDF (for formers)**
- **Approx. 3mm (⅛in) thick rubber sheet**
- **'G' clamps and/or sash cramps**
- **Bow saw**
- **Bandsaw**
- **Small circular saw or radial-arm saw**

STEAM BENDING
- **100mm (4in) plastic drainage pipe**
- **Exterior grade plywood (for bungs)**
- **Chipboard or MDF (for formers)**
- **Sash cramps and/or 'G' clamps**

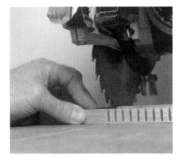

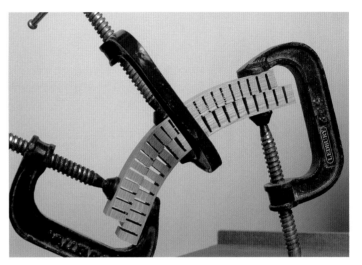

Radial-arm saw kerfing

1 A strip of narrow board is prepared to size (see Squaring Wood, page 54) and mounted on the radial-arm saw table against the fence. Place a pencil or ballpoint pen mark on the fence about 10mm (³⁄₈in) from the saw blade cut. This is the spaced distance between saw kerfs.

2 Set the radial-arm saw blade height just short of cutting all the way through the wood. Draw the saw head across and make a series of cuts, moving the wood each time and aligning the previous cut with the mark. The depth of cut may need adjusting to get the required bend. You can see how effective this simple method is but remember the saw cuts have taken the strength out of the wood.

3 By gluing and clamping two saw-kerf bends with their cuts inwards you can create an interesting structure, albeit with limited strength, in certain applications (see Veneering, page 114).

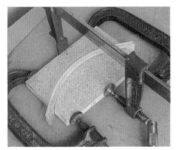

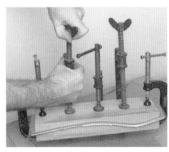

Laminating

1 Construct a male and female mould, allowing for the thickness of the entire laminated structure, which means the curves follow two different radii. Cut some laminates (see Sawing, page 44) 3mm (⅛in) thick in ash or beech and mix up some synthetic glue and apply to each laminate. The laminates are clamped in the male and female former using a sash or quick-release clamp to close them up.

2 'G' clamps are now added to pull the former in tightly. This jig demonstrates a simple radius but of course other curved forms can be achieved by this method. This is the basic principle of structural wood laminating and the resulting structures are very strong. A plastic sheathing has been used here to prevent the laminates from becoming stuck to the former. After the laminates have fully cured, the edges are trimmed with a plane.

Laminating using veneers

1 Usually beech constructional veneer is used with a more decorative facing veneer. Constructional veneers are thicker than normal veneers. The bends can be fairly tight because the veneer is pliable. In this simple former thin protective plastic sheet is used to avoid glue sticking to the former. Apply a thin coating of glue on to one side of the veneers.

2 Now clamp the veneers in the former with 'G' clamps, taking care to align the male and female parts of the former perfectly. The laminated veneers are left to cure overnight in a warm environment.

Steam bending

1 Build a former using plywood, chipboard or MDF to the desired shape and thickness. You can cut large holes to accommodate 'G' clamps. Make a bending strap from thin steel sheet and anchor it into the handles with bolts and screws.

2 For steaming the timber you will need a steam generator, such as a pressure cooker (shown here), and a steam chamber, which can be a plywood box or piece of plastic drainpiping plugged at either end with wooden discs. Into one end a tube enters carrying a constant source of steam. It is important to insulate the steam chamber to keep the temperature as high as possible. Here the drainpiping is insulated with kitchen foil and fibreglass roof insulation.

3 Wooden bungs are made for the ends of the steam chamber, which is mounted at a slight downward slant for condensed water to escape at the end into a bucket.

4 At the feed end (with its bung removed) the timber is stacked on spacers ready for steaming. Replace the bung with the hose entering it. Switch on the steam generator controlling the heat setting, so that a constant supply of steam passes through the chamber (escaping from the drainhole at the other end). As a rule of thumb, 45 minutes is needed for every 25mm (1in) thickness of wood to be bent.

5 After the wood has been steamed you must quickly transfer it to the bending jig, strap it in and make the bend in one go. Some trial and error is required to get it right. The steel strap helps avoid fibre break-out.

6 Now secure the jig with 'G' and sash clamps and allow to dry for several days.

Microwave bending

1 A domestic microwave cooker can be used to heat small sections of wood sufficiently for subsequent bending and forming in male and female moulds. The method takes some experimenting with.

2 It helps to keep the wood moist by wrapping it in a stout, sealed polythene bag with a little water in it or wrapping it in a saturated cloth. The microwave cooker is set at its 'high' position and timed for 3–5 minutes for a bend of about 3mm (⅛in) thickness. After microwaving, the wood is quickly placed in the former and clamped together and left for a few hours to fully dry out.

Shaping Wood

Often the tree itself is naturally shaped and curved and yet when the board is sawn and planed it becomes straight. This imposition over nature is arguably a long cry from the nature of the tree, but for economic reasons the straight cut is advantageous.

Much furniture today is, however, 'flat panel' work made from composite board such as chipboard or MDF with curves 'introduced', minimising the waste of this valuable resource.

It takes time, often several hundred years, for the shapes and curves of a tree to form, and so too it takes time to produce curves in the process of working wood. Shapes and curves add great interest to a piece of furniture and history is full of examples of the extravagant and skilful shaping of timber. The styles vary greatly from individuals such as the 18th-century woodcarver Grinling Gibbons to the present-day designer John Makepeace.

Curved and shaped work is also characteristic of specific craft traditions such as boatbuilding and musical-instrument making. Indeed entire cultures express the bendiness of the natural tree in their furniture traditions, such as the Scandinavian tradition of wood laminating and steam bending (see Bending Wood, page 98).

Wood can also be shaped or curved by coopering, bricking, stack laminating, saw kerfing or simply cutting to shape from solid timber. The age-old practice of searching for the right piece of timber that presents the natural structural curve is still in our consciousness despite the evolution of shaping techniques, especially those whereby the curve is imposed on the grain of the wood. A highly efficient modern sculpting tool is the power carver – a rotary version of a chainsaw.

CHECKLIST
- **Abrading sticks**
- **'G' clamps**
- **Pair of compasses**
- **Steel rule**
- **Sliding bevel**
- **Paper**
- **Scissors**
- **Glue**
- **Flat and convex spokeshaves**
- **Carving gouge**
- **Bevel-edged chisel**
- **Block plane or smoothing plane**
- **Coping saw, jigsaw or bandsaw**
- **Power carving tool (such as an Arbortech)**
- **Health and safety (pages 8–9)**

Power carving
A power carving tool such as the Arbortech is a highly efficient way of both shaping and finishing wood. The resharpenable cutting blades can be used for sculpting wood as well as applying a surface texture. The blade can be swapped for a sanding disc for finishing, making this a useful and versatile tool.

Imposing curves or shapes on to the grain
1 Most curves in woodwork are imposed on to the grain as opposed to following it, but you still have to observe the nature of the grain to obtain adequate strength. Here the piece will be weak at the top where the grain is very short.

2 In this hoop with the grain running vertically, the ticks indicate adequate grain strength and the crosses indicate weak or 'short' grain. When introducing curves in a piece of woodwork, try to avoid short grain as the wood is likely to break along it.

3 A simple and economical way to introduce a curve at the end of a straight piece is to glue on an extra piece, ensuring the grain matches. In the example above, the shaded portion and cutaway section show the intended shape.

Shaping with a spokeshave

1 Imposed curves can be easily marked out (see Measuring and Marking Out, page 38) and cut with a variety of saws (see Sawing, page 44). Finish with a flat-bottomed spokeshave, working in the direction of the arrows to cut with the grain and holding the spokeshave between fingers and thumbs. Rotate the workpiece in the vice to ensure you are always cutting more or less horizontally.

2 A convex-bottomed spokeshave can be used to cut concave shapes. You can also achieve a fine finish by abrading (see Abrading, page 104). Note the arrows indicating the change of cutting direction to go with the grain.

Making a coopered shape

1 Coopered work involves the segmenting of identical pieces to form a part or whole circle. First mark out the segments by scribing two concentric circles, dividing them into the required number of segments and converting the curved sides into two flat sides. With a steel rule and sliding bevel, the relevant data is transferred to a length of wood.

2 The wood is then planed (see Planing, page 48) and sawn (see Sawing, page 44). The angles are obviously critical in the marking out and cutting. Glue the segments together (see Gluing, page 66). A rubbed joint should suffice; it is not necessary to clamp them. Leave the segments to dry on a flat papered surface to prevent the assembly from sticking to the bench.

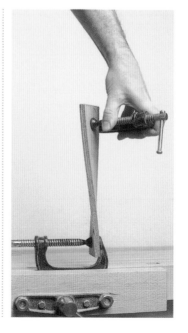

Shaping three dimensionally from a solid piece of wood

1 This curved stool or table leg can be easily sawn to a rough shape, having first marked the lines on two adjacent surfaces. The bandsaw is ideal for this task.

2 Hold the leg in a vice or clamp it to the bench (see Clamping and Holding, page 42), then shape with a spokeshave or carving gouge. Hold the gouge like a chisel (see Chiselling, page 56) and pare away the fibres working with the grain. Always keep the gouge razor sharp (see Tool Maintenance, page 32).

Twisting wood to form shapes

Twisting wood is a novel way of shaping; experiment using thin solid timber or plywood. Here a few layers of thin plywood have been clamped and turned to demonstrate the simplicity of the method. A simple jig can be improvised to hold the clamps in the desired position (for example, a length of wood in the vice can be clamped to the upper clamp). The twist maintains adequate pressure if a fairly liberal coating of synthetic glue is used. Such decorative twists can be veneered either before or afterwards to give the appearance of a solid piece. Clean up the edge using a spokeshave or abrading stick.

4 Alternatively a plane can be used. In this method the end grain is showing so you will be planing across the grain and hence the fibres will cut willingly. For ease of working rotate the wood in the vice, keeping the plane more or less horizontal.

5 The inner curve can be finished off by abrading or using a firmer gouge. You will find that a good way to finish the inside is to wrap some coarse abrasive paper around a shaped stick and work horizontally.

3 When the joints are dry, mark a line and you can then trim the outer edge by a variety of means. Here a chisel is used with the grain but you can also abrade the curve (see Abrading, page 104).

Brick and stack laminated constructions

1 Brick construction has numerous applications. Traditionally it is used to create curves for bowed drawer fronts that are veneered afterwards (see Veneering, page 114). The technique involves marking out the required curved segment, then tracing or transferring the data on to a piece of wood, which acts as a template for marking all the bricked pieces.

2 The pieces can be cut on the bandsaw and then glued together using a rubbed joint or by clamping if you feel this is necessary. The more accurate you are in sawing to the line, the less trimming you will need to do afterwards to finish the curve evenly.

3 Stack laminating involves the vertical gluing of any identically shaped pieces of wood. It can include plywood, in which case the ply is also a decorative feature.

Abrading

Abrading is the general term applied to smoothing wood flat prior to applying a finish but it is also a term for shaping wood using hand or power tools. Although much abrading does consist of sanding for a fine finish, it would be limiting to confine the term to this function only, since abrading is also an important shaping technique. There are many instances when other tools cannot easily fashion the wood. For example, in instances when chisels or planes might split the grain or when a saw is used to cut out the desired profile roughly and the general shaping and finishing is done by abrading.

Abrading involves the wearing away of wood fibres by the multiple sharp-toothed action of an abrasive material such as glasspaper. It also refers to the action of files or rasps and specific power tools and their accessories.

In some instances both hand and power-tool abrading methods can be used, although the latter is generally quicker and more efficient.

At the heart of most abrading is abrasive paper, usually a sheet or roll on to which the abrasive particles are bonded. The particle sizes are graded as a 'grit' and these are numbered. Generally you work through the grades starting with a coarser grit and working through to the finer ones until the wood is smooth and there are no visible sanding marks.

CHECKLIST
- **A range of abrasive papers**
- **Soft blanket or cloth for protecting work when finishing**
- **Cork sanding block**
- **A range of workshop-made abrading sticks**
- **Disc-sanding table attachment**
- **Power drill, eg 550 watts**
- **Orbital sander**
- **Belt sander**
- **Power carving tool with sanding disc (such as an Arbortech)**
- **Health and safety (pages 8–9)**

Hand abrading – shaping with an abrasive stick
1 Tear off strips of abrasive paper to the required size using a steel rule. Tearing 'freehand' is messy and wasteful.

2 Wrap the abrasive paper around a workshop-made timber forming block, creasing the edges back on themselves to form a sharp edge that clings to the block.

TYPES OF ABRASIVE

Abrasive paper
Glasspaper Useful in carpentry/joinery for general finishing.

Garnet paper Preferred by cabinet makers and fine woodworkers because of its excellent finishing properties.

Aluminium oxide A good all-round abrasive and particularly used with powered abrading.

Silicon carbide Mainly for metal but useful on some hard lacquers and finishes used on furniture.

Steel wool
Main grades used in woodwork are No.1, No.0, No.00 and No.000. Mainly used tor smoothing down between sanding or for the application of wax in the finishing process.

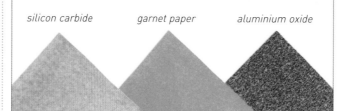

silicon carbide   *garnet paper*   *aluminium oxide*

ABRADING CHART

grade	grit		applications
very coarse	50	1	heavy shaping
	60	1/2	
coarse	80	0	shaping – belt, disc, orbital and hand abrading
	100	2/0	
medium	120	3/0	shaping and finishing – belt, disc, orbital and hand abrading
	150	4/0	
	180	5/0	
fine	220	6/0	finishing – power and hand abrading
	240	7/0	
	280	8/0	
very fine	320	9/0	final finishing, taking off sharp edges, sanding in between coats of lacquer – hand abrading
	360		
	400		
	500		
	600		

3 Hold the workpiece in the vice and use the abrasive block or stick like a file, preferably with both hands, cutting across the fibres. Change the abrasive strips when they begin to lose their bite and clog up with waste (especially when abrading resinous woods).

4 You can easily make different profile blocks or sticks to abrade curves and angled profiles. Improvised materials such as a short length of plastic piping can serve as an accurate former for concave abrading. You can use it like a file with fingers at either end to help stabilise the action, which goes across the grain, weakening the fibres.

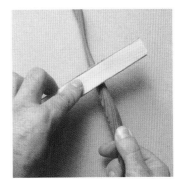

5 The abrasive stick method is very versatile. Here one hand abrades while the other hand rotates the workpiece.

6 You can work a thin strip of coarse abrasive paper 'bath towel' fashion to form circular sections accurately.

Using a hand-block
1 A cork hand-block is normally used for flat work. Mount the paper on the block, secure the workpiece in the vice or on the bench and apply firm pressure, working along the grain. More pressure and control can be achieved with both hands on the block. Use 120–180 grit paper.

2 When the grain runs the other way, try to sand with the grain, otherwise scratch marks will show.

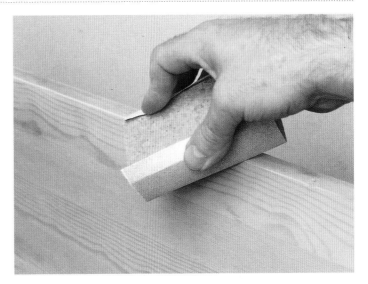

3 Generally speaking, wooden objects should not be left with sharp edges. A final finishing procedure is to 'soften' all edges with a fine abrasive paper (400 grit).

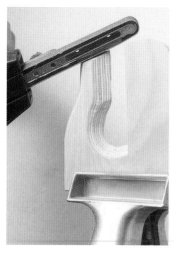

Power abrading – shaping

This narrow-belt power abrading tool can fashion wood fast and furiously. First secure the workpiece in the vice. The tool needs firm control directed at its tip, where it generally does the work.

Shaping and finishing using a power sander

1 A disc-sanding table attachment for a power drill is useful and accurate for angled or curved end grain abrading. Ensure the workpiece is fed into the rotation of the disc. This means that the rotation of the disc should push the work downwards on to the bench and not try to flip it up.

2 The table can be angled upwards and a bevel fence used on its face as a guide for compound angles. This is where an angle runs off at two planes rather than one.

Using a mini power carver

Mini carvers such as the Arbortech can be used with a sanding disc attachment. The angled head of the tool and small disc make this a handy option.

Using a belt sander

1 A belt sander has a continuous 75 or 100mm (3 or 4in) wide belt passing over a flat bed via two rollers. It abrades faster than other power sanders and the tool has to be held firmly to avoid it snatching and taking off.

2 The belt is changed quickly by a release lever that slackens the tension. Tracking is adjusted by a knob.

3 A belt sander can be inverted for flat and curved sanding. Ensure it is clamped to the bench and the workpiece held firmly as it is fed into the sander.

Using an orbital sander

An orbital sander is ideal for sanding large panels flat. Sanding sheets are attached to the cushioned oscillating baseplate. Let the weight of the tool do most of the work and keep it moving up and down and across the workpiece in gentle sweeping actions.

Scraping

The use of scrapers goes back at least as far as the Neanderthals. It is a primitive method of fashioning material and in particular wood. The action of a scraper is similar to that of a chisel, producing an extremely fine silk-like shaving. Because of this the scraper can be controlled to finish a surface delicately, especially where there is wild and irregular grain that might tear under a plane.

Scrapers produce a superior finish compared to abrasive paper, which can clog the grain especially when very fine grades are used. Any sharp-edged sheet material will serve as a scraper, even a piece of glass. Cabinet scrapers are quality steel and usually straight-edged, although there are different profiles for curved work.

The scraper is used particularly for finishing veneered work and – because of its ability to remove very fine slivers at a time – for removing excess glue. As a finishing tool it can be slow but its distinctive sound, like that of a spokeshave, expresses the true spirit of woodworking.

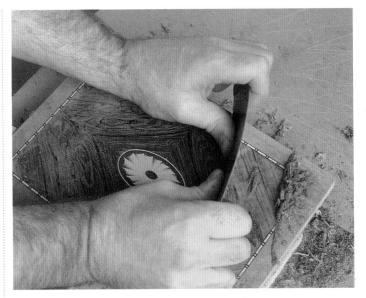

Using a scraper
1 Hold the scraper in both hands, wrapping the forefingers over the top edge slightly and pressing with the thumbs behind to flex the blade so that it curves away from you.

2 The amount of flex and angle of contact with the wood can influence the behaviour of the scraper, so you might find it useful to experiment a bit.

3 For localised scraping, such as for trimming flush the inlay banding on this veneered panel, the tool is bent more severely.

4 Try to work with the grain or diagonally and avoid abrupt strokes across the grain that could tear the fibres.

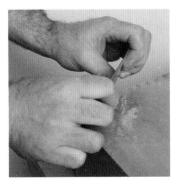

5 Using a scraper on solid wood is a traditional method of final finishing. For the best results sharpen the scraper frequently (see Tool Maintenance, page 32).

Turning Wood

Turnery is one of the simplest techniques in woodworking and it has enormous universal appeal. People are fascinated by watching wood being shaped on a lathe because the effect is immediate and the shapes alter so quickly. It is possibly one of the easiest techniques to learn, though to master it well there is no short cut to experience.

Anyone can learn how to use a lathe, which is a quiet, relatively inexpensive power tool that takes up little room, needing only a bench for mounting.

On the lathe you can turn small functional objects such as bowls, platters, goblets and decorative items, as well as make turned components for furniture such as chair and table legs.

The principle of lathework is simply that the workpiece is rotated at speed in a holding device such as a chuck, and these come in various shapes and sizes to suit the type of work being undertaken.

A variety of differently profiled scrapers or gouges are carefully fed into the rotating wood against the firm support of a toolrest, which acts as a stationary lever. These chisels or gouges are hand-held and moved by the operator to cut various shapes. The final finish can be achieved on the lathe, either straight from the tool, by sanding (see Abrading, page 104), by burnishing with shavings or by applying a wax as the work rotates. These techniques are explained in the following demonstrations. As lathework creates dust and chippings that fly everywhere, protect your eyes and lungs with an appropriate mask/visor.

Most timbers lend themselves to turnery and some especially so, such as pine, yew and elm; the latter is often turned 'wet' – that is, as unseasoned timber still containing a high degree of sap.

Turnery can make use of offcuts that otherwise might be too small to use. Turning wood is a mesmerising activity and once taken up will give endless hours of satisfaction.

CHECKLIST
- **Woodturning lathe or lathe attachment and power drill**
- **Set of scrapers**
- **Set of gouges**
- **Abrasive paper**
- **Calipers**
- **Tenon saw**
- **Hot-melt glue gun**
- **Screws**
- **Drill and screwdriver**
- **Health and safety (pages 8–9)**

Faceplate turnery: turning a bowl
1 Cut a bowl blank either octagonal or circular (see Sawing, page 44) and attach it to the faceplate by drilling pilot holes and screwing in place.

2 Mount the faceplate on the threaded drive spindle and rotate it by hand, aligning the toolrest and toolpost so that it does not foul – that is, so that the wood can rotate without touching any part of the lathe. Now set the toolpost for height – in line with the centre of the wood.

Faceplate work with a scraper
Although a gouge tends to be used by professionals, a scraper is also effective. Indeed it is easier to use although less efficient as a cutting tool. There is a wide variety of scraper profiles. Here the lip of the bowl is scraped flat. The toolrest is lowered so that the top of the scraper is in line with the centre.

Checking the depth of a bowl
A simple method for checking the depth, and hence avoiding cutting through into the screws that hold the bowl to the faceplate, is to use a straight-edge with the tool squeezed against it. Then transfer the screws to the edge where the thickness of the bowl blank can be judged. This is why short screws are used on bowl blanks – and lots of them for maximum anchorage.

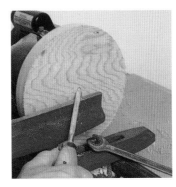

Using a gouge for faceplate turnery

1 The gouge is the most efficient tool for cutting wood on the lathe. Hold it firmly with both hands, tilting the gouge at an angle so that the tip engages with the wood. Switch the lathe on and feed the gouge gently into the wood, resting the bevel of the tip on the wood first, then lifting the handle to engage the tip with the wood.

2 The profile of the outer edge of the bowl can be cut using the gouge. The lathe speed can be raised from slow to medium as the bowl becomes perfectly circular and hence balanced. Make sure the gouge is kept razor sharp by frequent grinding (see Tool Maintenance, page 32).

3 Now move the toolrest around to turn the face of the bowl. The height of the toolrest should be adjusted so that when the gouge is tilted the tip is in line with the centre. Begin gouging out the inside of the bowl, feeding the horizontal edge of the gouge tip forwards.

4 The action usually starts at the centre and works outwards. A finer finish can be achieved after the roughing-out has been completed. As you remove more stock, you can move the toolrest closer, but only when the power is switched off do you make adjustments to the tool post; always take care to do this as a lathe can be very dangerous.

Finishing

1 Work through the grits from medium-coarse to medium, holding the abrasive paper between the fingers and applying it against the rotation and slightly below the centre. If the bowl is large, refrain from using the highest lathe speed. This should be reserved for spindle work, because it is safer.

2 Both hands can be used. If you press too hard you will soon know because the abrasive paper will get hot. Keep the abrasive paper moving to avoid the grit forming 'channels'. It is advisable to link up some form of dust extraction system when sanding as the dust is thrown centrifugally and can be dangerous if inhaled.

3 A handful of shavings can be fed against the rotating bowl. Some woods are more resinous than others and thus create a fine lustre to the workpiece.

4 A wax can be applied while the work is spinning but for lacquers or oils it is best to rotate the workpiece by hand. This is because lacquers and oils are much thinner than wax and would tend to be splashed about. Here olive oil is being applied to the bowl, highlighting the grain.

Turning between centres: spindle turnery

1 This method is applied to spindle turnery. Sometimes spindle work can be very small, such as for bobbins. First prepare the wood either octagonal or square in section; cut two 'V' grooves on one end, diagonally opposed, to find the centre of the wood, and drive in the fork centre with a mallet.

2 Mount the work on the lathe with the tapered end of the fork centre slipping into the hollow mandrel. This centre is called the drive centre.

3 Move up the tailstock and tighten and then screw in the end centre into the wood, first marking diagonals to locate the centre. A live centre rotates with the wood. A dead centre relies on friction and needs tightening frequently as it wears when turned. A little wax can be used on the dead centre to avoid friction burning.

4 Now set the toolpost to position and adjust the toolrest for height and parallel alignment. Rotate the workpiece manually to check it clears – that is, it does not touch the toolrest.

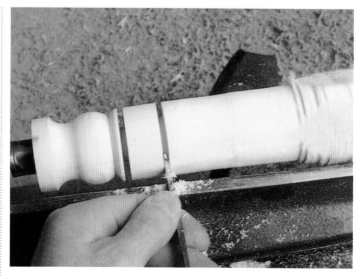

Scraping hollows

An appropriately profiled scraper is used to cut hollows.

Feed the scraper in gently. Frequent grinding keeps the tool cutting efficiently (see Tool Maintenance, page 32).

Scraping convex 'beads'

To shape convex 'beads' use a flat scraper or chisel, sliding it in a horizontal arc against the toolpost to form the curve.

Cutting slots and 'parting off'

Either a parting off tool or a narrow chisel can be used. The tool is driven into the rotating work, either for slotted features for decoration or for partially cutting off last of all.

Spindle work with a gouge

Tilt the gouge at an angle, holding the handle firmly with one hand and rocking the gouge through the fingers and thumb of the guiding hand. Fast stock removal comes with practice as one edge of the gouge drives horizontally across the work.

Using a scraper for spindle work

1 After setting the toolrest so that the top of the scraper is in line with the centre of the wood when held horizontally, feed the scraper gently into the revolving workpiece. The speed can be stepped up as the work becomes circular and properly balanced.

2 A wide chisel can be used as a scraper as it becomes a self-guiding jig for flat cuts.

Using calipers

Calipers are used to check the diameter of the work, first setting them with the aid of a steel rule. The work should be stationary when using calipers.

Hot-melt glue gun method

This novel method by the author offers a quick and easy way of attaching the workpiece to the wood-lined faceplate for small work, such as goblets and eggcups. Draw concentric circles on the faceplate to help position the workpiece accurately. Turning can create heat, so take care around the glue line.

1 Use a hot-melt glue gun to fix the workpiece on to the faceplate. The wood has to be perfectly dry and flat at the end. When starting to turn, the tailstock can be used for extra support. The advantage of the method is in turning the end and tool access. Of course there are a number of chucks that achieve the same result as this improvised method.

2 After the end has been fashioned you can then turn the sides to a slender profile. Notice the parting off cut that will be done last of all – after sanding.

3 The turned object is sawn off with a tenon saw when the lathe is switched off. With experience you can completely part off small objects on the lathe and it will simply fall into your hand as it is released.

Fretwork

There is probably no better introduction to the world of woodworking than fretwork, especially for youngsters, for it is a creative, enjoyable and basically safe pastime. Fretwork is a gentle and delicate technique in which wood as thin as 1.5mm (1/16in) can be intricately cut, usually to a prescribed pattern, template or line, for decorative or functional applications. It is probably true to say that 90 per cent of applications are decorative, although many toys and jigsaw puzzles are also made by this technique. The fretsaw also has applications in engineering patternmaking where it is often used to cut non-ferrous metals.

Nowadays the electric fretsaw has superseded the hand fretsaw and its quiet reciprocating action makes it one of the safest machines to use.

Compared with most other woodworking saws, the fretsaw blade is fine-toothed (there are numerous tooth options) and is easy to install in the machine. The fretsaw can cut all manner of curves, some extremely tight, in woods up to 20mm (3/4in) or 30mm (1 1/8in), and some machines have tilting tables enabling angled cuts up to 45 degrees to be made. The fretsaw is generally specified by its throat capacity. This is the distance between the blade and the back of the machine measured across the flat of the cutting blade. A machine with a 406mm (16in) throat could, for example, cut across a workpiece 812mm (32in) wide, if the operator reversed the workpiece end-for-end during the cutting process.

CHECKLIST
- **Assortment of thin materials (plywood etc)**
- **Powered fretsaw**
- **Selection of blades**
- **Health and safety (pages 8–9)**

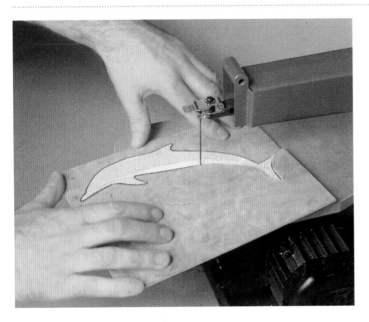

Powered fretwork using thin wood

Draw, trace or paste the desired shape on to a piece of thin plywood, such as 3mm (1/8in) veneered plywood. It is easier at first to use thin wood with a fine-toothed blade that can cut tight corners. Sometimes if the corner is too tight it is a good idea to back the blade out of the cut and to start another cut from a different angle. Look at the ventral (bottom) fin of the shark and you can see how difficult it would be to turn in such a tight spot. If you started another cut in line with the top edge of the fin, you could come right up to the body and cut away the waste quite easily.

Insert the blade with its teeth pointing downwards. The wood will want to snatch up, so hold it down firmly while you are cutting. Keep your fingers clear of the blade and blow away the dust as you cut. Many fretsaws nowadays are fitted with blowers that clear away the sawdust while you are working. These normally consist of a small plastic tube fixed near to the blade and connected to bellows operated by the up and down movement of the saw arm.

Powered fretwork using stout wood

1 To fret stout wood, such as 18mm (¾in) plywood, use a medium-toothed blade. This is because it has a more robust cutting job to do and is thus less likely to break in thicker timber. Holding the wood firmly down, slowly feed the wood into the blade. You can sense the speed of cut by the sound and feel. Never try to force the rate of feed into the blade. At best the blade will overheat and at worst it will break.

2 Cut tight curves slowly; again this is to avoid overheating and blade breakage. The finish left from the fretsaw blade is remarkably smooth, which is a great advantage in toymaking where delicate little fingers will become involved with the finished article.

Working enclosed cuts

When making an enclosed cut, for example one that does not come to the edge of the workpiece, there is obviously a problem in getting the blade initially to pass through the wood. This is done by first drilling a hole in the part of the wood that is to be removed, then disconnecting the blade at one end in the saw, threading the blade through the hole and reconnecting it. As always you should shade in the part to be cut out to avoid mistakes. It is remarkably easy to cut away the wrong bit, especially when working on complicated patterns.

1 For enclosed cuts, remove the blade from the fretsaw by slackening the tension adjuster. Then feed the blade through the hole you have drilled in the workpiece and reattach it to the fretsaw ready for cutting.

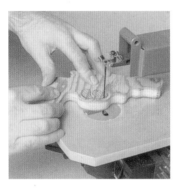

2 Hold the workpiece down securely and carefully cut to the line. Check your fingers are always away from the blade.

◀ JOHN ANDERSON
BOX

This intriguing box, which is made of jelutong (lime), is bandsawn. The outline of the box is drawn on to the wood and a slice removed. The box section itself, the 'hull' of the boat, is cut out with a fretsaw. The outline slice is then glued back on the original block and the profile cut out. The process is repeated to form the drawer section. The box is finished in acrylic paints, a shellac seal and a wax finish.

Veneering

Veneering is one of the oldest woodworking techniques, dating back to before the Egyptians. It is also one of the most relevant techniques of modern times as it is an extremely efficient way of utilising timber. A veneer is a wafer thin piece of the tree; in fact modern veneers measure about 0.6mm in thickness, which is about ¹⁄₅₀in. That is the equivalent of a piece of stout paper.

Veneer is glued on to a groundwork such as chipboard or MDF, typically a tabletop. If a tabletop 30mm (1⅛in) thick is made of solid wood, it is easy to calculate just how many veneered tabletops could be made from the same piece of timber, even allowing for wastage in cutting.

Veneered work is often associated with cheap furniture, and indeed much mass-produced veneered furniture does not last, but then the same can be said of much mass-produced solid wood furniture.

Veneering throughout the history of furniture making can boast some very fine examples of craftsmanship and has often been used to demonstrate the sheer beauty of wood. Equally veneer has been used to disguise shoddy workmanship and cheap constructions purely for visual effect.

The advantage of veneer is that it gives the cabinet maker a great deal more timber species to choose from. By restricting some rare species of timber for veneer cutting only, it has conserved those species or at least extended their life. Engineered or reconstructed real wood veneers are also used today, together with dyed veneers.

Modern veneered work overcomes many of the problems of timber movement associated with solid wood constructions, although early veneering was laid on to solid pine with inferior glues, leading to splitting and peeling off. Today chipboard and MDF are an excellent base for veneered work because of their stability, and this coupled with superior glues such as PVA make it a technique that is appropriate in terms of conservation as well as being useful, reliable and relatively inexpensive.

CHECKLIST
- **Ballpoint pen**
- **Steel rule**
- **Craft knife**
- **'G' clamps**
- **Hammer**
- **Scraper**
- **Router**
- **Health and safety (pages 8–9)**

Veneering a lipped panel
1 Select a piece of veneer slightly larger than the lipped groundwork (see Edge Treatments, page 118). Use veneer tape to bind any splits in the veneer by taping the outer side. Place the lipped panel over the veneer mounted on a backing board and mark the perimeter.

2 Using a steel straight-edge and a sharp marking knife, carefully cut the veneer about 3mm (⅛in) outside the marked line. It is important to cut across the grain first as this is most likely to split.

By using the marking knife at a shallow angle with the forefinger applying firm pressure, the action is firm and slow, especially at the end of the cut where the grain is likely to break out. The blade at this point is almost horizontal.

Vacuum pressing
1 Portable vacuum presses allow the home woodworker to achieve a professional result. Sandwich the veneered panel between two sheets of paper, then two boards slightly oversize, with rounded edges to avoid puncturing the bag. It can be difficult to check alignment once the panel is in the bag, but taping at the edges of the veneers can help with this.

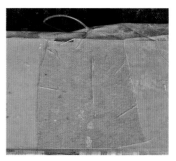

2 A breather fabric is supplied with the bag – position this so that air can be sucked from the sandwich to the pipe connector. Check the veneer alignment, then seal the bag and switch on the pump to remove the air from the bag. This creates sufficient atmospheric pressure uniformly over the piece to bond the veneer to the groundwork.

3 Now prepare a flat clamping caul: get ready some 'G' clamps and place paper under the groundwork; apply PVA glue with a spatula. Sometimes groundwork is 'keyed' (roughened up) with a toothing plane or saw edge but it is not necessary with modern glues. The spatula here is serrated to help spread the glue evenly.

4 The PVA glue is left to dry for a few minutes to allow water to evaporate before the veneer is placed over the groundwork. This is to avoid glue stains coming through the veneer or excessive water buckling the veneer, which is still possible even when it is under pressure in the clamped caul.

5 Mount the veneered panel against one or two flat cauls and clamp up so that the pressure is even. Allow to dry overnight or at least two hours under pressure at 15.5°C (60°F).

6 When the veneered panel is dry, the oversize veneer is carefully trimmed with the marking knife against a backing board. Tilt the panel with a spacer to transfer pressure at the knife cut.

The veneered panel is now ready for sanding (see Abrading, page 104) or scraping (see page 107).

Veneering a curved surface with impact adhesive

1 Curved work, especially larger work, is normally veneered using curved formers or cauls and a PVA or synthetic glue under pressure. For smaller work, impact glue is both quick and convenient, but it does tend to shrink over time. Select a piece of veneer to be glued to the curved work and cut it slightly oversize with the marking knife and steel rule.

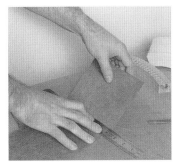

2 When cutting veneer you can cut halfway through, then break the fibres by lifting the veneer against the straight-edge for a clean cut. Use a spatula to apply the impact adhesive thinly on both surfaces and allow to dry for a few minutes. Always remember to replace the lid of the glue container immediately after use to prolong the life of the glue.

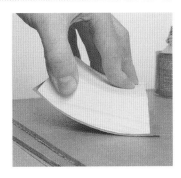

3 As both surfaces are brought together, the bond is instant. On larger work, a paper spacer can be used to help align the veneer with the groundwork. Press down hard against a flat surface.

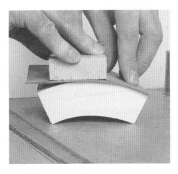

4 A pressing block can be used by hand or with the aid of a hammer to ensure perfect contact between the veneer and the groundwork.

Veneering adjacent surfaces on curved groundwork

1 The convex surface of the groundwork can be carefully trimmed with the marking knife, ensuring support is given to the fibres at the point of the knife cut.

The concave surface is more tricky and the veneer overlap may need paring back with the knife, taking care not to split the fibres.

2 An abrasive sheet can help to finally flatten the surfaces, ready for veneering.

3 Glue the veneer with an impact glue as previously described and trim afterwards with the marking knife against a backing board.

4 A hammer and scrap block can help bond in the veneer.

Clean up using an abrasive block and make the edge slightly radiused so that the thickness of the veneer is not apparent.

Applying an edging strip to a curved surface

1 This also applies to straight work but the principle is that two adjacent veneered surfaces may need reinforcing with small solid wood edging, which, in contrasting timber, can add visual interest.

Use a router (see page 60) with fence and straight cutter to rout a small rebate around the curved edge to accommodate the edging strip.

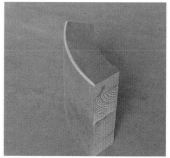

2 If the curvature is fairly gentle, the edging strip can be glued in place using masking tape as a clamping method. More severe curves can be achieved by pre-bending the edging strip, for instance by microwave heating (see Bending Wood, page 98).

Once the glue has set, remove the tape. Abrade the edging or scrape it flush with the veneer, which is then ready for finishing.

Applying veneers, motifs and bandings to a flat panel

1 Interesting effects can be had by laying veneers. Here a small panel is quarter matched and bandings added. Cut the veneer using a marking knife and backing board and use the veneer sheet as a marker for the other pieces required.

2 Very carefully trim, join and trim the four matching pieces using veneer tape. Also tape any splits in the veneer. Replace any severed pieces with veneer tape. Veneer tape is dampened (you can lick it) and is removed easily by further dampening after the panel has been glued.

3 Decorative motifs can be purchased in a variety of shapes, sizes and patterns. This oval motif is laid on to the centre of the quarter veneered panel with its paper backing uppermost.

4 Carefully cut through the veneer by tracing with the marking knife on a backing board. The motif is fitted inside the opening, taped down and glued with the panel using paper, cauls and clamps. The groundwork is cut large to accommodate a banding strip.

5 To border the veneered panel, a cross banding is cut with the grain running 'shortways' for decorative effect. Cut the strips of veneer for the cross bandings, joining with tape where necessary to achieve the desired length. First trim the edges of the veneered panel to form a parallel border around the panel. The mitres can be cut by laying the bandings in situ and carefully cutting through both together. Glue cross bandings separately using veneer tape and flat cauls.

6 Narrow strips in varying patterns of short-grained timber sections can add enormous visual interest to a veneered panel.

After the cross bandings have been glued and dried, the veneered panel is ready for inlaying the stringing. Using the straight fence, a router can be used to rout a very fine groove around the panel (see Routing, page 60). Take great care with narrow cutters as they are very fragile. The depth of the groove is just under 2mm (¹⁄₁₂in).

7 The radiused corners of the routed grooves are straightened up with a chisel (see Chiselling, page 56). Carefully cut the string by marking the mitred joins with a chisel. Then cut the stringings to the marked line against a backing board.

Use a veneer spatula to apply a little PVA glue into the grooves and carefully inset the stringings. A pin hammer can be used to press the stringings into place.

8 After gluing, the panel is ready for the satisfying part – cleaning up; this is best done with a cabinet scraper (see Scraping, page 107). First the veneer tape is moistened with a damp cloth and then scraped away to reveal the beauty of the wood underneath. The scraper is used in all directions but take care to work with the grain or diagonally to maintain a smooth cut. Although veneer is very thin, it is remarkable how it stands up to being scraped. The panel is now ready for finishing.

Edge Treatments

In much period furniture the edges of timber panels (for example, carcases, shelves, tabletops) were seldom left plain or 'square' but were profiled in some way to add visual interest. These sometimes ornate profiles are called mouldings and they also serve to soften the edges for more comfortable handling. Mouldings are also often put on to other timber artefacts solely for aesthetic reasons, such as in the case of picture or window frames.

Today there is a practical need for treating the edges of furniture for both tactile and visual reasons, especially as much of it is made of veneered chipboard. The brittle edges of this cheap substitute for solid timber need reinforcing with solid wood strips called 'lippings'. This can be done before the panel is veneered, so that the edges blend in discreetly with the face veneer, using the same material for the lipping. Lippings are usually at least 6mm (¼in) wide, offering scope for moulded profiles similar to those used in solid wood construction.

Traditional mouldings used to be cut with differently profiled handplanes, and there is an interesting vocabulary of profiles such as carvetto, ogee, cove, reed and astragal. Many of these planes are now collectors items and woodworkers of all ages are keen to acquire them for largely sentimental reasons.

Present-day routing technology has, to a large extent, replaced the old moulding planes and a vast range of profiled router cutters for shaping edges is used instead (see Routing, page 60).

(see Routing, page 60).

CHECKLIST
- **Measuring tools**
- **Abrasive paper**
- **Glue**
- **Masking tape or clamps**
- **Smoothing or jack plane**
- **Router and cutters**
- **Health and safety (pages 8–9)**

Types of edges
1 The simplest edge is a 'square' edge and this can be achieved with a handplane or by machine planing.

A SELECTION OF APPLIED AND CUT MOULDINGS

Some of the many traditional mouldings used in cabinetry that can be bought from most good suppliers. They can of course also be cut in the workshop with a router.

carvetto　　*astragal*　　*quadrant*　　*cove*　　*rute*

chamfer　　*reed*　　*cyma reversa*　　*ovolo*　　*bead*

Modern profiles tend to be less detailed and, generally speaking, fewer in number; again they are available from most timber suppliers.

The same router cutter can be used for these profiles, depending on where it is set in relation to the work. The curve in both cases is identical.

2 If you want to make a thicker board look thinner or more delicate, plane a chamfer (or slope) along the bottom edge, first using a marking gauge and then planing to the line.

3 All edges of furniture should be slightly softened with very fine abrasive paper. This removes the sharp edge, which is known as an 'arris', and is both soft on the eye and the hand.

Using a router to make moulded edges

1 A variety of moulded edges can be achieved by using the router and fence, set up with a profiled cutter. It is sometimes hard to visualise a profile because it is the exact opposite of the shape of the router cutter. When in doubt, simply make a final cut on a piece of waste timber and if you like the shape use it.

2 Some router cutters have ball-bearing guides and can therefore follow concave and convex edges. Afterwards you need to finish the moulded section with abrasive paper.

Applying lippings to a veneered panel

1 Make sure the edges of the manufactured board are true and square. This is very simply done with a try square, but do make sure that the stock of the square rests firmly against the surface of the board.

2 Prepare to size some 6mm (¼in) wide lippings, which should be fractionally thicker than the chipboard. Mitre the corners (see Mitre Joints, page 76) and then glue and tape the lippings in position on the edges.

3 With a handplane, trim the lippings flush, ready for veneering. Work inwards to avoid splitting the grain. After the panel has been veneered the edges can be profiled as though they are solid wood, provided the lipping is wide enough.

Hinges and Locks

Some advanced woodworkers devise ingenious ways of opening cabinet doors or locking the lids on trinket boxes etc, without resorting to proprietary metal hinges, locks or catches. A poor quality mass-produced hinge, or crudely designed handle, will certainly let down an otherwise finely crafted cabinet.

Most woodworkers, however, whether beginners or highly skilled, will resort to standardised fastening hardware, of which there is now considerable choice for most applications. Choose a fitment to suit the job. For example, if you are building a wardrobe door a pressed steel or brass plated hinge that is simply screwed on to the surface might be adequate, but if you are making a delicate trinket box a precision-made cast-brass hinge would be called for.

Visual appeal, strength, durability, size and specific function are important factors to consider when choosing the right hinge, lock or catch.

Once the choice has been made you should then select the best tools and woodworking techniques to attach the ironmongery accurately. As you develop your woodworking skills, you will find that being able to hang a door correctly or to fit a lock that engages properly is both satisfying and extremely useful

CHECKLIST
- **Pair of small brass butt hinges with appropriate countersunk (CSK) screws**
- **Marking gauge**
- **Marking knife**
- **Combination square**
- **Sash cramp and packing pieces**
- **Small screwdriver**
- **Drill bits**
- **Chisel**
- **Mallet**
- **Tenon or dovetail saw**
- **Coping saw**
- **Power drill and shank and pilot bit**
- **Router and small straight cutter**
- **Health and safety (pages 8–9)**

Using a router to cut a hinge recess
1 One method of cutting a hinge recess is to use a router and straight cutter (see Routing, page 60). The marking out techniques used for sinking a hinge by hand (see opposite) can be applied or the hinge can be offered up to the router cutter to establish the depth of the recess. Making a trial cut in a piece of waste wood is another way of establishing the depth for the recess.

2 One drawback with using a router is that the recess will always finish with curved ends, which have to be removed with the chisel (see Chiselling, page 56). The final step is to trim the ends of the recess across the grain to the line.

Using a router to cut a lock recess
1 A router set up with a straight cutter can be used to cut the fine recesses using the same techniques as with the hinges.

2 To remove the bulk of the lock recess, plunge the router in a series of overlapping cuts, setting it to a depth-stop. Final trimming to the curved ends is done with the chisel in the same way as cutting hinge recesses.

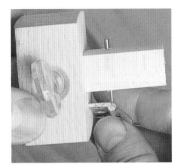

Sinking a brass hinge into a small casket

1 Mount the casket firmly on the bench. A sash cramp held in the vice with an appropriate packing piece is convenient. The packing piece between the cramp head and the casket is to avoid bruising or marking when the cramp is tightened. The hinge lengths are first marked out on the wood with a sharp marking knife. Their positions can be guessed; each one should be nearer the end of the casket than the middle, but do ensure they are both the same.

2 Using a try square, lightly square the lines across the wood to the approximate hinge width and down the edge to the approximate hinge thickness.

3 Set a marking gauge to width using the hinge itself. Note that the spur (or point of the gauge) is set to the centre of the pivot of the hinge. This action is repeated for gauging the depth of the hinge recess. This is very important and ensures the lid and box faces meet exactly.

4 Gauge the width of the hinge recess using the locating points that you marked originally, to prevent overrun of the gauge. Reset the gauge to mark the depth of the hinge recess and repeat the process. Now deepen the squared cut lines to where the marking gauge lines intersect and shade in the waste.

5 Now mark the opposing hinge lengths on the lid by carefully extending the lines so that the hinges will align perfectly. Then repeat the marking out operations.

6 With a mallet and chisel carefully sever the waste fibres across the grain by a series of fine parallel cuts, say 2mm (¹⁄₁₂in) apart. Work from the centre moving outwards in each direction, carefully locating the chisel for each cut.

7 Now work the chisel horizontally to lift out the severed fibres. After the fibres have been severed across the grain (see Chiselling, page 56), carefully pare the fibres back to the line along the grain.

8 The final step is to trim the ends of the recess across the grain to the line.

Inserting hinges

1 Insert a hinge and mark off the centre hole with a pencil. Then drill a pilot hole fractionally nearer the shoulder (where the long edge of the hinge will butt against) to ensure a tight fit when screwed in.

2 After cutting all four hinge recesses, run a finely set plane along the edge to produce a slight bevel. This enables the lid to swing freely.

3 Now screw the hinges in position, using the correct width screwdriver to avoid scratching them. In tough woods use a steel screw as a 'primer'. This means a steel screw is inserted first to widen the pilot hole. Brass screws are much softer and would be likely to break when driven into hardwoods.

4 Drill the pilot holes for the remaining screws.

5 Now insert the remaining screws. It looks much neater if all the slots are in line or on the same diagonal.

6 When the box closes the faces should meet with no more than the clearance of a thin piece of paper to allow for the thickness of a coating of lacquer at the finishing stage. If the hinge recesses have been accurately marked out to start with (see Measuring and Marking Out, page 38) and then cut out with care, perfect alignment should result. Note that the hinge knuckles protrude slightly.

7 Any fractional misalignment can be rubbed down with an abrasive block on the front and side edges to bring them level.

Fixing a mortise lock
1 The various recessed parts of the lock need to be marked and cut in stages. First place the lock on to the wood to mark out its overall outline.

2 The marks are squared across with a combination square and marking knife in a similar manner to marking out for the hinges.

3 Use the adjustable-depth try square facility of the combination square to extend the lines downwards.

4 Use a tenon or dovetail saw to cut across the grain to the line on the side and edge.

5 Mark off the various features of the lock by holding it against the wood.

6 For the shallow recess, chisel out the waste horizontally across the grain.

7 In such a confined space, the trickiest part is to cut an accurate line along the grain at the bottom of the lock. Here the bevel of the chisel is used to give a vertical cut.

Keyhole location
1 Mark out the keyhole position using a marking gauge and try square to transfer the information from the lock.

2 Drill a slightly oversized hole for the keyhole. Using a coping saw, insert the blade into the hole, then carefully cut the keyhole verticals, finally trimming with a narrow chisel.

3 Now insert the lock into its recess and check that everything is flush. In this confined space, use a nail with its tip flattened as a screw pilot hole.

4 Fix the lock with fine screws, and check the key for operation when the catch plate has been attached.

5 The catch has to be very accurately recessed into the lid so that the key operates smoothly. The catch will sit flush (level with the wood) in the lid. Mark out its profile with a try square and marking gauge.

6 Recess the catch using the same methods as used for sinking the hinges.

7 Drill pilot holes and fix with fine screws, ensuring everything is perfectly flush.

8 A fine bevel can be run along the edge with a smoothing plane as a continuation of the hinge bevel for visual effect.

▶ ROBERT INGHAM
CASKET

As many as 80 small panels of burr elm held in frames of bog oak are used in the construction of this casket. The lining and trays are of ripple sycamore. The hinges are also made of wood, while the brasswork fittings are designed and made as integral elements of the overall design.

▼ MARTIN LANE
DIAMOND HUMIDOR

A small object of desire, this beautifully crafted humidor (cigar box) celebrates wood in its veneer form, including amboyna burr, ripple sycamore and Macassar ebony, with ebony and holly inlay. The interior has two chambers for cigars; the central element holds accessories. Within the lid there are humidification units. The hinge is in two parts: the pivoting part is a bought hinge, in brass for strength; the quadrant part, which acts as a stop, is handmade in brass for strength. Both hinge parts are heavily silver-plated and polished to a mirror finish.

Finishing

Most objects in wood usually require a protective coating of some kind, depending on their function and environment. This coating is invariably known as a 'finish'. It greatly enhances the visual appeal of a piece of furniture, and different timbers demand different finishes such as lacquers, oils, waxes or stains. Finishes can be applied by pad, brush, roller or spray.

In some cases it is better to leave the timber in its bare natural state. Some Danish furniture in the past has been left bare and by subsequent scrubbing with soap solution a natural lustre has evolved. When woodturning a hard wax can be applied to the rotating object or the wood burnished with shavings (see page 109).

Arguably a highly lacquered finish acts as a barrier to the natural material and this can be a drawback, especially as wood is a warm tactile material. But generally it is an advantage to apply some kind of lacquer or oil to give a protective coating to the wood.

Some woodworkers believe that the wood should always 'breathe' and that a fine oil or microporous lacquer should be applied; others would prefer to totally seal the wood, which helps inhibit timber movement due to the loss or intake of moisture in the air. Conventional lacquers can be up to 40 per cent impermeable whereas epoxy resin coatings are up to 100 per cent impermeable and

can withstand excessive heat. Finishing is both science and art, and you should never be afraid to experiment.

Today, solvent-based finishes are increasingly being replaced by water-based finishes that are arguably not quite as tough but safer to use. Adherence to health and safety is paramount if using solvent-based finishes, not least in ventilating your workspace and wearing a mask with the correct filtration.

Prior to finishing, the workpiece should be filled if there are knots, holes or blemishes, then sanded smooth by hand or power sander (see Abrading, page 104). All marks should be removed, with edges slightly softened, or rounded, with the abrasive.

CHECKLIST
- **Proprietary wood filler, fine abrasive paper and block**
- **Polishing pad and cotton**
- **Variety of soft brushes**
- **Acrylic lacquer**
- **Cellulose lacquer**
- **French polish**
- **Wax polish**
- **Very fine wire wool**
- **Soft burnishing cloth**
- **Polyurethane varnish**
- **White spirit or turps**
- **Danish oil**
- **Linseed oil**
- **Wax oil**
- **Water stain or spirit stain**
- **Two-part epoxy resin**
- **Health and safety (pages 8–9)**

Preparing the surface
1 Whatever finish you are using, surfaces need to be carefully prepared. In this sequence a wood filler is made up from sanded dust from the item to be lacquered, mixed in with a drop of cellulose lacquer. In this way you can always be sure that the colour is right. A fine wood spatula helps to work the filler into any knot holes or blemishes.

2 After filling any unsightly holes, lightly abrade the surface with a 400 grit abrasive paper block.

3 Remove any residual dust by blowing or by using a dry brush. In this case the dust has to be removed from a fine groove in the lid of the jewellery box.

Applying acrylic lacquer with a pad or brush

These steps also apply to using a cellulose lacquer or French polish (such as for antique refinishing). Acrylic lacquer is a fast-drying convenient finish, available in gloss, satin or matt. It can be applied with a brush, pad or aerosol spray. When brushing, it is a good idea is to use a lacquer jar and to make a plywood brush holder that also acts as the lid to prevent the lacquer from hardening, especially on the brush. A pad can be easier to control. The pad is made of wads of cotton wool wrapped in a piece of cotton or linen.

Equipment and brushes should be cleaned with water when using acrylic lacquer, but for solvent-based lacquers use a proprietary thinner.

1 Having prepared the surface, load the pad with lacquer and partially drain away the excess against the lip of the container.

2 Work the pad swiftly in circular motions across the surface. Note how the beauty of the grain is enhanced and how the wood takes on a rich lustre.

3 Then work the pad lightly along the grain and parallel to the edge. The knack is to apply a little lacquer quickly and build up two or three coats with an interval of a few minutes.

4 The entire box can be finished in one operation. If you apply the lacquer very thinly, it will be touch-dry in seconds. After two coats of lacquer have been applied – with 20 minutes between coats and an hour to harden finally – the lacquer can be de-nibbed (lightly rubbed down to remove any small rough spots) with 400 grit abrasive paper or wax polished with a fine wire wool.

Applying a wax polish

You can apply waxes directly to bare wood but ideally the grain should be sealed by lacquering first. Not all woods should be waxed – open-grained timbers can attract dirt and are best left varnished.

After preparing the surface, dip a small wad of fine wire wool into the wax polish and lightly rub it into the grain, finishing with the grain direction. Finish with a soft dry cloth to polish the surface to a lustre.

Applying epoxy resins

Epoxy resins that cure (or harden) by heat with a chemical catalyst are extremely hard, durable and water and chemical resistant. They come in two separate containers and need to be mixed shortly before use. They are commonly known as 'two-part' adhesives. They can also withstand very high temperatures and are almost totally impervious.

After mixing the epoxy with its catalyst in a mixing container, apply it thickly with a brush. You should take care to avoid runs on vertical edges. The epoxy must be left to cure for at least a day and then rubbed down between coats. To achieve an immaculate finish you will find it is necessary to apply several coats, rigorously rubbed down with fine abrasive paper between.

French polishing with a pad

French polish (also known as white polish and button polish) is a quick-drying 'traditional' finish that is thinned with methylated spirit. It is softer than cellulose lacquer and is applied in several coats with half an hour or so between them.

Prepare the surface and then apply the french polish with a pad, similar to the application of cellulose lacquer. Apply a little polish using a fast circular motion.

Applying an oil finish

Suitable oils, such as linseed, danish (or teak) or wax oil, are applied by brush or cloth. Oils are particularly suitable for exterior woodwork as they are water repellent and they give an excellent lustre to certain woods. As oils are absorbed deep into the fibres, it can help to thin the first coat by up to 20 per cent white spirit.

Applying a polyurethane varnish with a brush

This is a durable general-purpose lacquer available in solvent-based (white spirit) or water-based gloss, satin or matt finish, suitable for interior and exterior woodwork.

Generally two or three coats are desirable. To obtain a deeper penetration, thin the first coat by up to 20 per cent using white spirit. Polyurethanes take about 2 hours to dry (6 hours between coats) and allow you a few minutes 'working time'.

1 First you should 'break in' a new brush by roughing it against a clean stone surface. This will make it flexible and also get rid of any loose hairs that might otherwise spoil the finish. Dip the brush into the varnish and wipe off half of it against the edge of the varnish container.

2 Now brush the varnish quickly and evenly across the workpiece. You do not have to go with the grain initially.

3 After the entire surface has been saturated with varnish, brush lightly at a shallow angle parallel to the edges to avoid drips and runs.

Applying a wood stain

1 Wood stains are generally oil- or water-based, the former being easier to apply and the latter deeper penetrating. Alternatives can be used effectively. Subtle colour-fast applications of artists oil paint, for instance, can be used, followed by a turpentine-based lacquer. Start by preparing the surface. Apply a water stain with a pad or brush. Subsequent wiping off with a damp cloth can improve the consistency of the finish.

2 A black stain is used to fill the open pores in this piece of ash. It is then rapidly wiped off, allowing the grain and figure of the wood to show through. This gives an ageing effect to the timber that many people find pleasing. It is a good idea to experiment on a piece of scrapwood of the same type first.

Applying a stained varnish

Polyurethane-stained varnishes can be applied by brush in exactly the same way as clear varnishes. A first coat of clear varnish can be applied or the stain varnish applied straight on to bare wood.

When applying a stain varnish to either sealed or bare wood, the final brush strokes should go along the grain. Two coats may be necessary.

4 Tilt the workpiece up (you will have to varnish the underside after the first side has dried) and work the brush lightly and swiftly along the grain, checking against the reflection of light for runs.

SPRAY FINISHING

Spraying is a quick and efficient method of applying finishes.

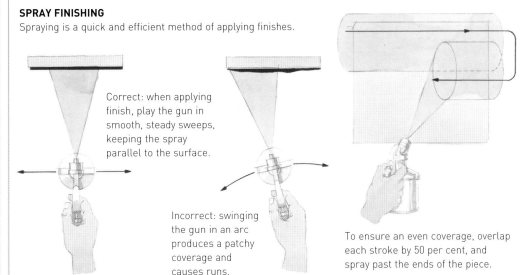

Correct: when applying finish, play the gun in smooth, steady sweeps, keeping the spray parallel to the surface.

Incorrect: swinging the gun in an arc produces a patchy coverage and causes runs.

To ensure an even coverage, overlap each stroke by 50 per cent, and spray past the ends of the piece.

Themes

Wooden objects are not only aesthetically pleasing, but they are often useful, and the imaginative expression of techniques in their making can be an important aspect of their function. Most pieces express a number of techniques, and whether a piece is intended to be a visual feast or a subtle understatement of form and material, the importance of techniques cannot be over-emphasised.

There is nothing more inspirational than to look at the work of the masters of technique. The objects illustrated in this section, which include tables, cabinets, chests, chairs and decorative items, have been chosen because they express some of the techniques described in the first part of the book and because they show some of the almost limitless possibilities that exist in their creative application.

◀ SARAH KAY
OWL TALLBOY
Made from solid French cherry, the sides, top and bottom of this tallboy cabinet are each built up of nine layers and shaped on a spindle moulder using a jig. All of the components are cut from the same section of timber (crown-cut boards) so that shrinkage/expansion is uniform. The doors are mitred with a hole in the centre, in which a geometric pattern is woven with waxed cotton. The back of the top section of the cabinet and the drawer linings are veneered with cork.

Cabinets and Chests

A cabinet or chest is usually a box with four sides, a back and some kind of lid.
Some cabinets are raised on legs to a more convenient practical height.
'Cabinetry' is a woodworking term that refers to a broad vocabulary of
techniques centring around carcase work and panel-and-frame construction.

The most common cabinet carcase is a four-sided solid wood box construction jointed together with dovetails. A cabinet can also be machine jointed and made of a veneered manufactured board such as chipboard or MDF. There is a lot you can do with a box construction to turn it into an interesting cabinet. A range of different joints, either exposed or hidden, can hold the box together at its corners. The doors can be hinged using different methods or designed to open, close and lock in a completely novel way. The internal detailing of the cabinet can introduce an inner wealth of craftsmanship and interest revealed once the doors are opened. Some cabinets are deliberately ornate and decorative, such as those of the Art Nouveau period; others are subtle and understated, often revealing an element of surprise. Some rely on a combination of woods for their visual appeal, or they reveal a fragrant woody smell when drawers are opened.

Drawer making is the high art of cabinet making, and the real test of a craftsperson. Curiously there may be plenty of 'different' chairs, tables and other objects, but when it comes to cabinet drawers, traditional methods are invariably preferred. The drawer has to be made with precision, so that it glides in and out, creating a 'piston' effect as it compresses the air within the carcase. Traditional drawers are time-consuming, and those masters of perfection are often masters of speed.

The cabinet employs the logic of much woodworking technique and the respective tools – flat panels jointed at right angles, parallel surfaces clamped together with ease and square edges checked with squaring tools. For this reason cabinet making is at the heart of woodworking, and indeed a cabinet is a pleasurable object both to possess and to make.

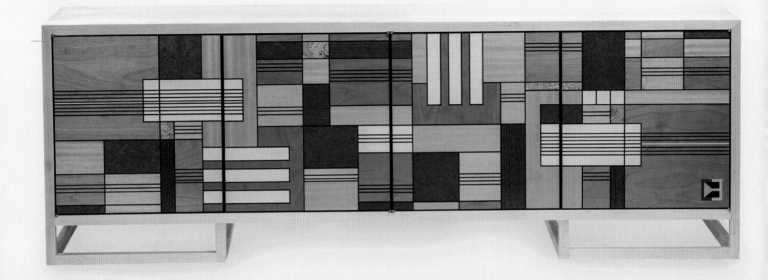

▼ **THOMAS WHITTINGHAM**
RIVEN SIDEBOARD

This sculptural sideboard has intriguing hidden elements – a whisky cabinet lifts out of the back of the cabinet on gas struts. The piece combines lamination techniques for the curves (using a male/female former) with biscuit-jointed carcase construction. The timbers used are birch plywood, figured olive ash veneer, figured ash veneer, ash constructional veneer and green slate veneer. There are four push-to-open drawers on mechanical runners and a cupboard space for bottles and glasses. The finish is wax oil.

◀▲ **CHRISTINE MEYER-EAGLESTONE AND CHRIS TRIBE**
GRID IV (LEFT) AND OPPOSITES: CIRCLES AND STRIPES (ABOVE) SIDEBOARDS

It is not often makers collaborate but it is usually exciting when they do. The carcase construction of these two sideboards is by Chris Tribe and the hand-cut marquetry by Christine Meyer-Eaglestone. Christine presses the marquetry design on to 18mm (¾in) MDF using a PVA veneer glue and passes the marked-out components to Chris for cutting and assembly. The 'Grid IV' carcase is solid maple; the marquetry is maple, dyed pama, birch, dyed tulipwood, engineered veneers and ebony edging. The 'Opposites' carcase is European oak fronted with American black walnut for the six drawers; the marquetry is maple, walnut, mahogany, dyed tulipwood, engineered veneers and ebony edging.

▼ TOM COOPER
ORCO DRINKS CABINET

Constructed using traditional frame and panel jointing techniques and domino joints, this curvaceous display or drinks cabinet is made of Scottish elm. The door is made from three alternating grain layers of solid elm (essentially a plywood construction using solid quarter-sawn elm to give the door strength and minimise movement), which is then shaped using a router and custom-made templates. Inset carcase sides are in burr elm and glass has been used in the door. The finish is wax oil and wax polish.

▲ ANTHONY AYLWARD
LADIES' JEWELLERY CHEST (CHEST OF DRAWERS)

This chest of drawers gives the impression of being a chest on top of a table. Made from solid maple with walnut inlay, it involves traditional joinery using mortise and tenon joints for the carcases and hand-cut dovetails on the drawers. The drawer knobs are walnut turned on the lathe. The finish is clear lacquer and beeswax.

◀▲ MARTIN HARVEY
FLOWER CABINET

With a hint of the Arts and Crafts movement in its design, this cabinet is fairly traditional in look and construction. It is an example of frame and panel work, with shelves and drawers employing housing joints and dovetails respectively. Designed for the management of everyday household paperwork, it is made from American black walnut with an inlaid abstract flower pattern of European oak and maple on the doors.

▶ MARK RIPLEY
ASH AND ELM CABINET

Designed for a home study, this cabinet is made from American white ash with elm drawer fronts and door panels. The panels are full length and the stiles are thick enough at 30mm (1¼in) to accommodate the panel and supporting frames. They also allow for comfortable inset handles, which are hand carved. The lower drawer fronts are from a single piece of elm, creating a visual flow though the drawers. A water-based lacquer finish is used to retain the lightness of the ash, with oil on the elm to accentuate the colour.

▶ TONY PORTUS
KANJI CHEST OF DRAWERS

The gently sweeping, form-defining elements of this piece were created in response to a brief to bring a lightness of touch to what is essentially a functional and capacious bedroom chest. Inspired by Chinese calligraphy, the sweeping lines are picked out in boxwood cockbeading and burr walnut, with tapering drawer handles following this design signature. Solid walnut drawer fronts open to reveal meticulously crafted oak drawers, dovetailed front and rear, which also feature solid oak slips and muntins to support the cedar of Lebanon drawer bottoms that bring their own unique and gorgeous scent.

▼ MARTIN HARVEY
SIDEBOARD

This sideboard is made from European oak with a decorative sycamore relief pattern set within a grid. Instead of wooden handles, simple leather tab pulls have been used for opening the doors. There is adjustable shelving within.

▶ ANDREW VARAH
SIDEBOARD

The classically flowing lines of this exotically veneered sideboard exhibit great, but subtle, attention to technical and visual detail. Because the fumed madrona burr veneered door fronts are likely to pull and, therefore, bow, the same kind of wood has been used as a balancing veneer on the other side.

▲ ANDREW LAWTON
BALLARD HALL COURT SIDEBOARD
Made of European oak with English walnut detailing, the solid wood carcase is jointed with hand-cut through dovetails and mortise and tenons. The doors use 3mm (⅛in) thick constructional veneers cut on a bandsaw and lipped on to an MDF substrate. The doors appear to hang between the bold fluted front rails. The corners are jointed with a mitred cross-halving joint. The client's brief was that visual impact was more important than maximising storage capacity. The finish is matt water-based lacquer.

◄ ANDREW LAPTHORN
CHARLIE CHEST OF DRAWERS

This engaging chest of drawers is made of solid maple with masur birch veneer. It combines several techniques, including solid carving for the top, laminating for the legs and turnery for the ebonised beech drawer handles. The finish is clear acid-catalysed lacquer finished with wire wool and wax.

▶ JOHN MAKEPEACE
WINGS CABINET

This commanding cabinet is made from a single tree of ripple sycamore, converted especially, and is almost as high as the crown, standing at 2.4m (8ft). It is elliptical in plan, with the shelves cantilevered off the curved back, from which the solid sycamore doors are hinged. The idea arose from the concept that the folds in the 'fabric' would be the handles. Although digital designing was involved, it is hand-carved inside and out.

▶ NICO VILLENEUVE
LIMED CABINET

This cabinet is made using architectural thickness veneer to allow the texture to be enhanced. Crown-cut oak is laid out and book-matched in a quartered pattern, and then given a whitened finish (liming) to bring out the dramatic grain of the wood. The tapering on the nickel-plated handles reflects the subtle angled recessing of the carcase front.

◄ CHRISTOPHER BURLEY
WALNUT CREDENZA
The solid carcase of this American black walnut cabinet is constructed using mitred corner joints with a partition and shelf inside. The design on the doors is routed with the grooves graduating inwards to give the illusion that the doors curve in towards the centre, adding a focus and delicacy to the robust dark carcase. The door design is inspired by Bridget Riley's painting *Loss*.

► CHRIS TURNER
CUBIST CREDENZA
With splayed legs reminiscent of the 1950s, this cabinet has been constructed using mainly traditional furniture-making techniques. The framework is mortise and tenoned, while the walnut carcase is mitre jointed using the domino system. The embellishment of the doors is achieved using hand-cut marquetry/parquetry techniques, with maple and oak veneers glued on to an MDF substrate in a vacuum press. The doors open with knife hinges. The finish is sprayed acid-catalysed lacquer.

◀ ANDREW LAWTON
BUREAU BOOKCASE

This cabinet is an example of 'frank jointing' in the spirit of the Arts and Crafts movement. The solid English oak construction includes oak veneered panels at the back. The main carcase is assembled with through mortise and tenons that are foxtail-wedged with walnut. The bureau section is through dovetailed. Interestingly the carcase is actually three separate carcases, emphasised by the use of the walnut 'waist' details and inlaid walnut squares. The finish is danish oil.

▼ ALAN PETERS
BLANKET CHEST

This functional bedroom storage chest expresses the honest construction of carcase pinned tenons slightly protruding through the chest sides with their radiused edges. There is a good reason for this – as timber shrinks and expands, the flush through tenons would not remain so for long. The beauty of the highly figurative Douglas fir, a softwood, celebrates material and technique.

Chairs and Benches

Aristotle was happy to sit on a boulder while thinking his thoughts and ever since then humankind has sat upon every conceivable thing. The chair is probably the most over-designed object in history and to this day it is still regarded as the ultimate challenge for designers.

The great architects of the world have tried their skills at designing chairs – Le Corbusier, Alvar Aalto, Charles Eames. It has been said that a designer's reputation can be made for a decade if he or she creates a new chair, but if it is comfortable then it is a bonus.

The wooden chair is particularly challenging as not only is the material appropriately tactile for such an object but the strength requirements can easily result in an over-engineered and visually confusing design, so the designer has to know the material well. To produce a wooden chair that satisfies the criteria of adequate body support, soundness of construction, simple, elegant, understated lines and a clear expression of technique and material is a tall order, and very few chairs pass the test.

A well-known designer once said, 'There has to be a very good reason for me to design a chair.' That reason is often to do with technique or technical revolution – a new way of using the material.

In this selection of chairs, classic designs have been included that are particularly significant from a technique point of view: Michael Thonet's 'café society' chair of the mid-19th century exploited wood bending; Alvar Aalto's laminated designs of the 1930s were inspired by trees bending in the wind; Hans Wegner's chair of 1949 employed a variety of techniques and successfully married handicraft traditions with industrial production.

Today 'designer' chairs tend to be more self-expressive and there is no major design style or technical innovation emerging that can be seen as coming anywhere near the importance of the above mentioned examples. But the challenge to produce new and interesting chairs is as great as ever and this selection shows a few examples of chairs that explore technique as a major part of their raison d'être.

◀ **HANS J. WEGNER**
CHAIR

Made of oak with a seat of woven cane, the flowing back and arms of this classic chair are an object lesson in wood shaping, while the overall construction relies on intricate joints. Originally designed in 1947, this chair is an example of Danish mass-produced articles based on the tradition of hand-crafted work. Note how the curved front rail enters the wider round-sectioned leg with a recessed shouldered mortise and tenon joint.

◀ **ALVAR AALTO**
CHAIR

This classically formed chair is a perfect example of bending wood. It was created in 1936–37 by Alvar Aalto, the famous Modernist designer, and produced by the Finnish company Artek, which was founded by Aalto and his wife. The bending of the sections of birch stretches wood laminating technology to the limit in the formation of the long, cantilevered shape, and the technique wholly dictates the form. Any decoration to enhance the timeless qualities of the design would be superfluous.

▶ **MICHAEL THONET**
CHAIR

This classic chair was designed by the German craftsman Michael Thonet, who was working in Austria in the mid-19th century, and it marked a milestone in the development of woodworking techniques. Its radical shape relies entirely on steam bending. The plywood seat, which may be up to 50mm (2in) thick, is formed in one continuous bend, which pushed the bending technique to the limit. Its superb visual lines, comfort and economic use of wood have made it probably one of the most copied chairs ever to have been produced.

▲ HANS J. WEGNER
CHAIR

The commanding lines of this superbly made ash and teak chair embrace several interesting techniques. Bending wood is used to achieve the laminated curve, while the shaped 'peacock feathers' enter the seat with dowel joints. The legs and cross rails use turnery. Although this chair was made in Denmark, it is in many ways similar to the classic English Windsor chair.

▼ JEREMY BROUN
STOOL

The inspiration behind this small stool or table is the Scandinavian tradition of bending wood. It is made from a continuous piece of ash, steam bent by means of a domestic kettle, and using routing techniques and simple jigmaking. The wood at the actual bend is reduced so that it can be shaped over a simple jig, but the bend is re-strengthened by the solid mahogany inserts, which are routed in diagonally using another jig. The resulting structure is routed away at the edges to expose the finger inserts and to enhance the form.

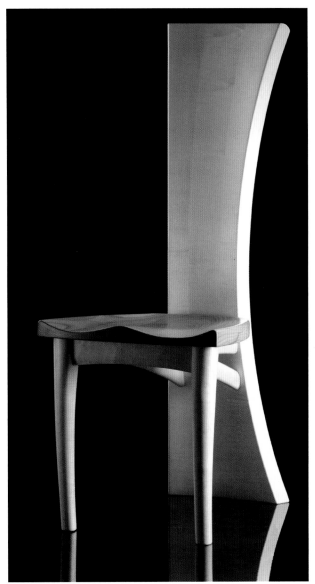

▲ KAREN HANSEN
SETA STOOLS

Three-legged stools are a classic theme and here the maker has played with the elemental geometry of spheres and triangles to create a fairly minimal and robust structure. Getting the balance right is difficult and this design shows how the structure of a piece can also be the aesthetic.

▶ SCOTT WOYKA
SHIPPON CHAIR

Originally commissioned as a set of 12 for a round dining table, this high-backed dining chair is designed for comfortable dining, with good back support and a shaped hardwood seat. An interesting feature of the design is the organic 'branched' seat rail, which gives the chair structural integrity in a distinctive and stylish manner. The rails are jointed into the back leg with a locking joint that, once assembled, cannot come apart. The materials are cherry with sycamore.

▶ **TOM VAUGHAN**
RIBBON CHAIR

This striking chair, designed by Tom Vaughan of the design and fabrication co-operative Object Studio, certainly pushes technique and form to the edge, resulting in a chair that is both comfortable to use and a piece of sculpture. The chair is carved from Arctic white maple and finished with a white-tinted hard wax oil, protecting the timber from everyday use as well as the aging effects of UV light.

◀ **FRED BAIER**
PRISM CHAIR

This series of prism-shaped blocks is composed in such a way that they become a chair with one arm. The quarter-sawn oak is sandblasted, leaving the medullary rays high. Each component is coloured with a dark stain and then the faces are sanded to remove the colour from the high points. Solid colour (paint) is then rollered on to that high ground rather like inking up a printing plate. Versions of the chair are in the collections of the Victoria & Albert Museum in London and the Carnegie Museum of Art in Pittsburgh, USA.

▶ KATIE WALKER
RIBBON ROCKING CHAIR

Achieving a chair design that says something new and looks great is rare. This elegant laminated chair involves twisting 1.5mm (¹⁄₁₆in) wood veneers bonded with epoxy resin to create the ribbon frame. The leather-clad seat has a laminated plywood shell, which is connected by a stainless steel rod framework with articulated joints threaded into the ribbon frame, resulting in a light but rigid structure of great strength.

◀ JOLYON YATES
SAVANAH III ROCKER

This rocker is a rare and beautiful example of simple form, functionality and structural integrity in a chair. Being made entirely of stack-laminated birch plywood, the inner beauty of this undervalued material is manifest in the far from simple construction, which is dependent on the unique bonded multi-directional fibres of this man-made material. Along with hidden volumes and voids, it lends incredible strength while allowing for the tuning of balance, strength and weight. The finish is water-based polyurethane. With a background in automative design, Yates has brought a fresh look to furniture construction and this piece is undoubtedly a modern classic.

◄ MARK RIPLEY
ROCKING CHAIR

This chair in ash, oak and black walnut was developed through a series of prototypes with particular attention given to the ergonomics of seat, back, arms and rocking action. The seat is coopered, glued in a series of bevel-edged blocks to an approximate shape and then routed to a fair curve using a curved trammel jig. This is the only jig used on the piece, which is otherwise mostly handmade apart from bandsawing the initial curves of the frame. The front edge of the seat is hand carved. Laminated strips form the back slats, which feature properly positioned lumbar support. The finish is wax oil.

▶ THOMAS WHITTINGHAM
GRIZEDALE CHAIR

This functional but stylish chair is made from rippled ash with olive ash and figured ash veneer; the seat is leather. The all-laminated parts are made in a vacuum press with a male former; the back is shaped later. The back splat is laminated from decorative veneer to maximise layers in a thin component. The finish is a low-sheen gloss lacquer.

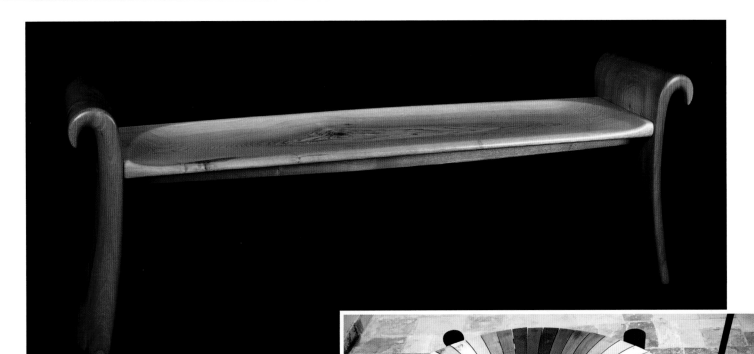

▲ SCOTT WOYKA
GARRICK'S BENCH
This bench, designed to sit in a hallway, is made from English elm and ash and utilises traditional through wedged mortise and tenon joints. Sawing from solid timber, shaping and spokeshaving are used to sculpt the elegant shape.

▶ ALICE BLOGG
SPECTRUM BENCHES
These three outdoor benches – two positioned side by side and the third opposite – are made of curved and shaped English oak slats on a patinated metal frame. The colours of the oak come from reacting or taking away the tannin in the wood, creating a spectrum of colours in a beautiful gradient. The benches form three-quarters of a 3.5m (11ft) diameter circle.

▶ TERRIE NOLL
BENCH
The designer of this magnificent Art Nouveau-style bench used electric carving tools to shape the intricately woven patterns in the mahogany. The finishing is, however, by hand abrading. The end panels are veneered in blistered mahogany.

▼ JEREMY BROUN
TILT ROCKER
Made from quarter-sawn English oak, this chair uses a car leaf-spring concept to obtain the rocking motion. A polyester-terylene pre-stretched cord is used for the novel upholstery.

◄ IAN BIRCHALL
URBAN COUNTRY CHAIR

Green woodworking is often
associated with rustic ash or
elm furniture, with natural splits
featured because the wood is
fashioned wet and will inevitably
shrink out. This more sophisticated
looking chair uses oak, ash and
maple and is fashioned using a
draw knife and spokeshave after
the members have been bent in
a steam box. The seat is woven
rush and the finish is oil.

▶ NAMON GASTON
OXBOW ARMCHAIR

This chair is made of laminated and solid
European oak, with an oak bark tanned
Swedish leather sling seat and back.
Keyhole-shaped profiles are cut into
the frame with a router for holding the
leather slings. The slings are hemmed
at each side and held in place within the
profiles with wooden dowel rods inserted
into the hems to lock the slings in place.

Tables and Desks

A table is a flat supporting surface at a given height depending on its function. The table has been described as the social centre of the home. It is where much learning occurs, views are exchanged and where social interaction takes place.

The conference table is usually larger and more prestigious in construction and form, and allows interaction in a more deliberately structured way – the circular conference table is 'democratic' as it allows all members to feel they are equal. The coffee table may be the only hand-crafted item in an interior full of mass-produced objects. It might be highly individual or quite plain and subdued.

The table offers a challenge to the woodworker. In order to achieve a supporting surface at a given height there are numerous construction options beyond simply placing four legs at each corner. Consider the problem in terms of a space to be filled by a structure that draws on a wide vocabulary of woodworking techniques. This is what makes designing so exciting – putting aside preconceptions about the way a piece should look or whether it should rely on traditional constructions. Instead you identify a series of problems, set down criteria that must be met and then consider the most appropriate techniques to use.

Some tables in this selection explore particular conceptual or technical themes of interest to those designers or perhaps the clients for whom the tables were intended. Some examples are relatively easy to make and others deceptively simple-looking. A table is an excellent object for a relative beginner because its main elements need only be a supporting structure for a flat top. The top could be made of MDF with its edges lipped and the legs could be of a standard section employing simple joints. However simple in form or construction your table is, it needs to be made well and the foundation of its success is the command of technique.

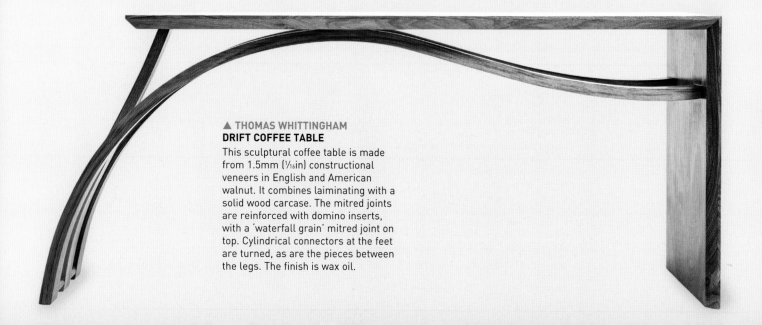

▲ THOMAS WHITTINGHAM
DRIFT COFFEE TABLE
This sculptural coffee table is made from 1.5mm (¹⁄₁₆in) constructional veneers in English and American walnut. It combines laiminating with a solid wood carcase. The mitred joints are reinforced with domino inserts, with a 'waterfall grain' mitred joint on top. Cylindrical connectors at the feet are turned, as are the pieces between the legs. The finish is wax oil.

▼ THOMAS WHITTINGHAM
OLIVE DRESSING TABLE AND STOOL

In an age of self-adornment, this is described by the maker as a large jewellery box. It has seven hand-fitted drawers lined with pig skin suede; one of the drawers is hidden for special items. With book-matched veneer work throughout and laminated curve work, the materials used are birch plywood, burr olive ash veneer and solid European ash. The finish is wax oil.

▶ **ALAN PETERS**
FAN TABLE
This elegant fan table is a masterpiece in technique and aesthetics, with perfectly sculpted flutings forming the tabletop. Each fluting is a separate tapered piece of timber, constructed in a jig and then jointed and glued together. Made of solid rosewood, it was intended for a hallway.

▼ **ANTHONY AYLWARD**
STEPPED POD TABLE
This deceptively solid-looking table is actually constructed from a series of mitre-jointed frames, glued and dowelled together. Each frame is offset to achieve a desired curve. It is made from Irish olive ash and finished with clear lacquer.

◄▼ CHRISTOPHER BURLEY
JOANNA WRITING DESK

This elegant but practical writing desk is a solid timber construction of American black walnut and maple. The three drawers are made with hand-cut dovetail joints and finished with curved handles cut from a continuous laminated piece of walnut.

▲ TOM COOPER
TIP-TOE TABLE

Made for an exhibition of handcrafted furniture utilising trees that had succumbed to Dutch elm disease, this side table is designed to reflect a tree's growth. The solid burr elm top is joined in three matching sections; the sycamore inlay details are routed and then finished with a chisel. The solid elm legs are fluted by hand using a custom scratchstock. The legs and tabletop are joined using loose tenon domino joints, glued with PVA and finished with wax oil and wax polish.

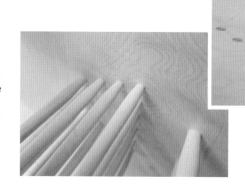

▶ JOHN EADON
MIMA SIDE TABLE

Deceptively simple in form, the drilling of holes at different angles to create the structure of this table involves great skill. Made from English sycamore, a further subtle detail is in the wedging of the spindle tenons as they enter the top. A PVA-type glue has been used and the finish is wax oil.

◀ TOM COOPER
EMBRACE COFFEE TABLE

Designed for the reception area of a hospice, this coffee table is intended to reflect a feeling of connection and comfort in its soothing, flowing curves, with the aim of being sympathetic to the people using the table when coming to the hospice to visit terminally ill family and friends. It is made from Scottish elm with reclaimed purpleheart details. Cut into 4mm (⁵⁄₁₆in) thick constructional veneers, the elm is shaped into the curved form in a vacuum press. The teardrop detail on top is routed and then hand finished with a chisel. The finish is wax oil.

▲ JOHN MAKEPEACE
RIPPLES DESK AND FITZWILLIAM CHAIR

These two visually powerful designs complement each other in form and celebration of material and technique. The rippled sycamore is echoed in the solid sculpted table end that cleverly morphs into a solid top. The pattern was developed on a computer to control the motion of a router, an evolving technology and an addition to the craftsman's vocabulary. The accompanying chair is the prototype for a pair acquired for the permanent collection of the Fitzwilliam Museum in Cambridge, and is made of aluminium and fumed oak with an aniline leather seat. The stunning cast and polished aluminium combined with the fumed oak is a striking marriage of materials.

▶ **DAVID TRAGEN**
BEATING WINGS COFFEE TABLE
An example of precise yet organic stack laminating, this table has a light feel despite its solid form. The American cherry structure is held together with a series of repeat halving joints. The edge of the plate-glass top is slightly curved to complement the curved wings of the base.

▼ **JOSHUA GABRIEL**
STINGRAY RIPPLE COFFEE TABLE
Pushing the boundaries of furniture is in our DNA, and this coffee table, inspired by the geometry of the helix coupled with the flow of movement, almost appears to float along. Made up of 73 laminates of sweet chestnut, it is shaped by hand with spokeshaves and scrapers. Only a quarter of the construction can be made at one time before the next section is clamped. The finish is a pigmented oil to create a whitewash appearance.

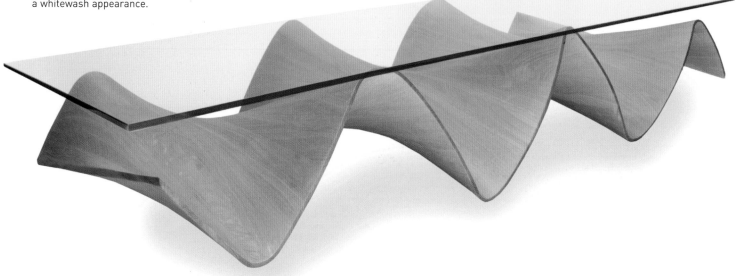

◀ **ROB ELLIOT**
SHORTHORN DESK

This beautifully sculpted desk and chair are made of Scottish elm using a brick construction. The aim was to create a practical and aesthetic desk inspired by the flowing curves of the grain in the timber. Powdered resin glue has been used and the finish is a sprayed water-based polyurethane lacquer.

▶ **KEVIN STAMPER**
STILL LIFE COFFEE TABLE

The tabletop design, inspired by a picture of a bowl of fruit depicted in a modern pixelated language, is created using individual squares (30 x 30mm/1⅛ x 1⅛in) of hand-dyed sycamore veneer on an MDF substrate. This tabletop is counterbalanced with a framework of fumed English oak. The finish is clear lacquer with UV inhibitors.

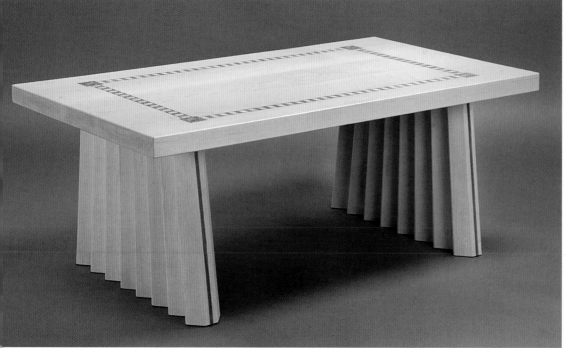

▲ CHRIS TRIBE
ORIGAMI COFFEE TABLE

The tabletop is made from jointed maple boards, with laminated elm, walnut and cherry inlay fitted into a routed groove. The fluted legs are formed by jointing tapered profiled sections. A short tenon almost the full width at the top of the leg is housed into a groove in the underside of the tabletop. The finish is acrylic lacquer applied with a felt pad and rubbed down to a satin finish.

▶ SARAH KAY
VIOLET VANITY TABLE

Made from solid ash, the hoop sections of the table are laminated using 2mm (1/12in) thick veneers glued around a former and then shaped round after drying. The mirror is glued to a plywood back and screwed into a rebate in the main hoop. The back leg terminates with a small dish made from turned ash and lined with leather. The stool seat is bowl shaped and has a matching leather seat that sits flush to the timber edge. The legs tenon into the seat without the need for wedges.

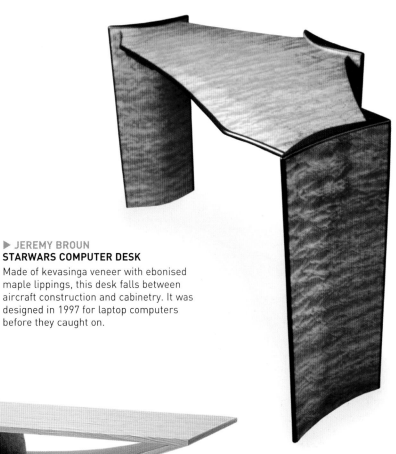

▶ JEREMY BROUN
STARWARS COMPUTER DESK
Made of kevasinga veneer with ebonised
maple lippings, this desk falls between
aircraft construction and cabinetry. It was
designed in 1997 for laptop computers
before they caught on.

▲▶ ANDREW LAPTHORN
ST JOHN'S ALTAR TABLE
The brief for this altar table
was that it should be light in
both weight (movable by two
able-bodied persons) and
appearance – to have an airy,
uplifting, see-through quality, as
opposed to the more ponderous,
monolithic altars of the past.
The table is made from olive ash
veneer (external surfaces) and
olive ash burr veneer (internal
surfaces) laminated on to a birch
plywood core using a vacuum
press and powdered resin glue.
The finish is a low-sheen
acid-catalysed lacquer.

Miscellaneous Woodwork

This section features a range of wooden objects, including pieces that are primarily decorative as well as those that simply fall outside the more clearly defined categories chosen for this book.

First, a word about decoration from a historical perspective. To decorate is to adorn or embellish with ornament. It is a term that tends to refer to the somewhat superfluous method of styling, notably of past work that at best includes highly skilled carving or fretwork and at worst can be a visual disguise for inadequate structure or inappropriate constructional technique. Decorative can mean veneered, painted, gilded, gessoed, Japanned and a whole raft of traditional surface treatments, some of which come under the title of *trompe d'oeil* (trick of the eye).

The term decorative has a more modern and broader connotation, referring to objects that are primarily designed to please the eye or generally stimulate the senses; perhaps objects whose main function is to adorn the functional environment. Although chairs, tables and cabinets are more clearly understood as functional or utilitarian objects, some examples are highly decorative or possess a sculptural quality. When talking of function it is limiting to consider just one function or purpose. A chair may be primarily for sitting on but visual appeal is extremely important too.

Some examples chosen for this section are highly decorative or possess a sculptural quality. Others explore new functions, combining with technology or drawing from technology. Other items are small and therefore make it possible to use rare timbers that would be less affordable in a larger item. Of course when looking at wood and its fashioning techniques, a musical instrument, and in particular an acoustic guitar, is a wonderful celebration of a variety of techniques and timbers.

Today, with the boundaries between art, craft and sculpture overlapping and the increasing interplay of hand skill with new technologies, the visual aspect in bringing alive our planet's oldest natural resource – wood – is ever more important.

◀ **TOM RAUSCHKE AND KAAREN WIKEN**
BOWL

This unusual bowl features a reversible top, one side of which represents a winter landscape, the other a summer landscape. The outer bowl shape is turned on a lathe from a solid hickory log, and then cut with a jeweller's saw before being hand carved to make what might have been a simple, functional container into a unique piece. The removable landscape cover is created using marquetry techniques. The summer fields are made from black walnut, lignum vitae, maple, Osage orange, ash and ebony, while the snow-capped details on the winter scene are made from holly. The lignum vitae trees are turned on a lathe before being milled on a drill press. Kaaren Wiken's embroidery of the reflected sky is contained under the glass-topped 'pond'.

▼ **JONATHAN LEECH**
NATURAL EDGE BURR SYCAMORE BOWL

Simple natural form and simple technique, this bowl in burr sycamore retains the natural edge of the chosen piece of the wood. Turnery is an example of a unified skill – one that involves a single wood-fashioning process. The piece is sanded and finished with lemon oil for a perfectly smooth finish.

◀ **MAX BAINBRIDGE**
STANDING VESSELS

These sculptural birch vessels are turned on a lathe until thin, so that as they dry they can move. The wood is also turned green, initially the day after the tree was felled, to encourage movement and cracking. Once dry, they are sanded to a fine finish and then burnished with a cotton polishing wheel to give a subtle lustre.

▼ CHRISTINE MEYER-EAGLESTONE
DAZZLE I MIRROR

'Dazzle I' features hand-cut marquetry using dyed tulipwood veneer as well as engineered wood veneer. A PVA veneer glue is used to press the marquetry design on to MDF. The mirror is edged with 5mm (³/₁₆in) thick sycamore hardwood. Christine creates unique hand-cut marquetry designs that play with spatial illusion, often through vibrant use of colour and bold geometric composition. Her designs evolve while intuitively choosing from a 'palette' of conventional and engineered wood veneers as she manipulates line, edge, colour and texture to generate compositions that can convey a sense of order and balance or one of vitality and tension.

◄ SALLY BURNETT
A COLD & FROSTY MORNING (ABOVE) AND RAVEN (BELOW) VESSELS, CORVUS NERO COLLECTION

These vessels are lathe-turned from end-grain 'green' English sycamore. Once dry, each vase is bleached several times to achieve the translucent, porcelain-quality surface. The feather design outline is carved into the wood using pyrography, with additional detail added using a micro drill with dental burrs. This textured surface is then coloured using matt black acrylic paint, with subtle iridescent highlights added using acrylic interference paint. The background is textured with a micro drill following the ghost of the grain that remains after the bleaching process.

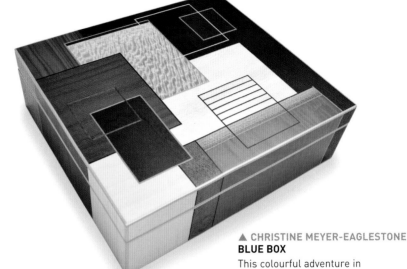

▲ CHRISTINE MEYER-EAGLESTONE
BLUE BOX

This colourful adventure in intersecting lines and rectangles almost suggests that the pieces fit together like a Chinese puzzle, but in fact this decorative box features hand-cut marquetry on its surface. It uses conventional, dyed and engineered wood veneers and there is a hardwood edging. On the inside the lid and base are lined with orange suede. The box opens and closes with discreet barrel hinges only visible from the inside.

◄ FRED BAIER
BOOK CHARIOT TROLLEY AND LECTERN

Made of quarter-sawn English oak for a coopered barrel and with CNC tube bending, this innovative piece was created for the House of Lords Library in London, reflecting the maker's experiences as 2011 Artist in Residence. To transport 3m (3yd) of books on carpet demanded big wheels, and the hubless concept was inspired by the *Tron* movie. Add a pinch of the 19th-century gothic revivalist architect Pugin, and this colourful piece has more than a touch of concentric about it!

▼▶ SCOTT WOYKA
PEBBLE BOX

A strikingly simple yet intricate casket in fumed chestnut and sycamore, the design was inspired by rounded boulders found on a beach. Inside is a tray in which to keep whatever you wish. The tray comes out, and you could hide some precious papers below. Dropping the tray back in, it floats down on a cushion of air, like a car piston, such is the tight fit. Techniques used include stack lamination and dovetails.

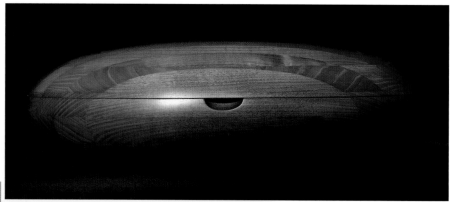

▶ CHRISTOPHER HAUTH
HALL STAND

Subtly blending the needs of form and function, this delicate hall stand is visually arresting. The low-key tung oil finish is in keeping with the fine lustre of the black walnut, and the traditional joinery employed reflects the simple nature of its application.

▲▶ JEREMY BROUN
DIGITAL TOUCHSCREEN JUKEBOX

Made from tiny 'planks' from a board of maple, this award-winning piece was designed in 2005, four years before the iPad emerged. When not in use a 2mm (¹⁄₁₂in) tambour with routed grooves is slid up to cover the screen, turning the jukebox into a sculpture. The adjustable pivoting head allows remote armchair viewing as it doubles up as a video kiosk. Tiny grooves are routed into the tapered carcase sections to enhance the 'plank' effect.

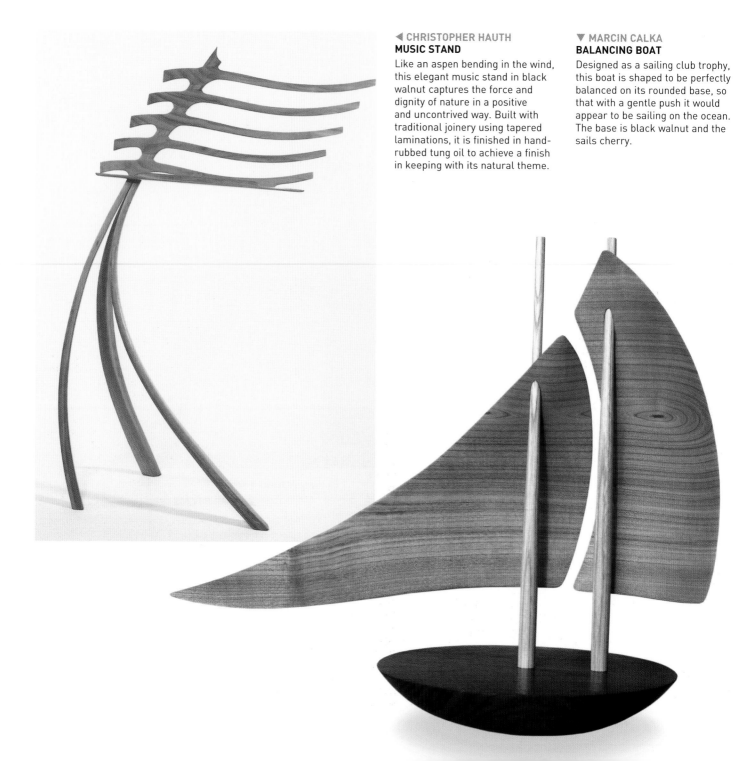

◀ **CHRISTOPHER HAUTH**
MUSIC STAND

Like an aspen bending in the wind, this elegant music stand in black walnut captures the force and dignity of nature in a positive and uncontrived way. Built with traditional joinery using tapered laminations, it is finished in hand-rubbed tung oil to achieve a finish in keeping with its natural theme.

▼ **MARCIN CALKA**
BALANCING BOAT

Designed as a sailing club trophy, this boat is shaped to be perfectly balanced on its rounded base, so that with a gentle push it would appear to be sailing on the ocean. The base is black walnut and the sails cherry.

▲ TOBIAS KAYE
SOUNDING BOWL

This sounding bowl in cherry is one in a series that Kaye creates by turning. When forming these delightful pieces, Kaye pays great attention to the 'acoustic curve', listening as well as using his eyes and hands to assess its harmony of form. If these acoustic bowls are to be successful, the thickness of the walls have to be one-eightieth or one-fiftieth of the diameter, depending on whether the bowl is deep or shallow. Strings are fed through brass tubing inserted in the bowl walls; this brightens the tone and prevents the strings from cutting along the grain.

◄ JEFF KEMP
GUITAR

The construction of a classical guitar embodies the greatest possible variety of woodworking techniques, from the edge jointing of the wafer-thin cedarwood face, the shaping of the underface struts and the bending by heat of the cocobolo rosewood sides, to the abrading of the sculpted neck and drilling of the head for the machine heads. Any luthier knows, however, that the moment of truth depends not on whether the joints are tight and the glue lines almost invisible – although these are important, of course – but on whether the instrument has the right sound when it is first plucked. Even then, the quality of the sound may depend on the finishing.

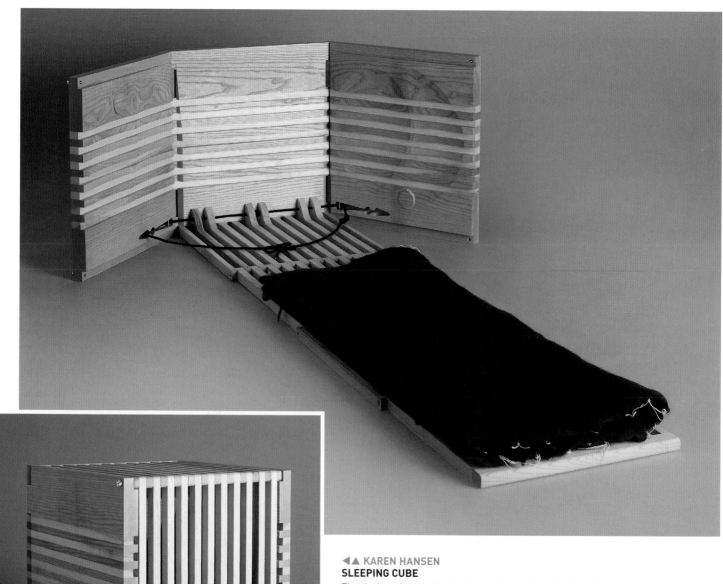

◄▲ KAREN HANSEN
SLEEPING CUBE

The design of this ash sleeping cube was inspired by the contrast between linear and organic forms and by the choice of tools used to make it. The advantage of the sharp cubic form is utilised in the folding mechanisms and as a module. The gentle flow in the organic form enhances comfort and the sense of safety. One cube unfolds into a cosy chair or a bed with headboard, and two together create a flexible snug corner. All makers are influenced by the tools available to them and this in turn affects the design process. Marked by hand or machine? In carving the nuanced cut comes directly from the handheld gouge, while the machine leaves a pre-programmed mark. The open cube shows the inside headboard panels made by the use of CNC routing.

◄ **DAVID ATKINSON**
THE CITY AND SKY BOX
A rich feast of rare and exotic timbers, this box is made up of laminates of European beech for the lid and black-dyed Swiss pear for the box. The veneers used for the marquetry overlay include Macassar ebony for the windows and night sky (with painted stars), burr ash for the moon and black-dyed Swiss pear for the windows; the buildings are made from imbuya, bird's-eye maple, satinwood, purpleheart, bloodwood, fiddleback makore, coffee tree, anigre and curly cherry.

▼ **DAVID BARRON**
DOVETAIL BOX
Perhaps the most iconic woodworking joint through history is the dovetail. A departure from the straight dovetail is the oblique dovetail used in this curved box. Made from bird's-eye maple and American walnut with a spalted beech tilt-top lid, the interior is lined with green padded pig suede. Angled dovetails are novel but more difficult to cut by hand than the standard dovetails. The finish is hand-rubbed melamine lacquer and then wax.

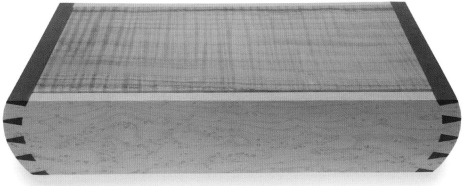

▲ **MARTIN HARVEY**
HEART BOX
Made from European oak with a decorative inset spline and heart motif on all four sides, this fun-looking box has a rebated lid that lifts off with a single leather tab handle.

Index

Credits

We would like to thank and acknowledge the following for kindly supplying images of finished pieces for inclusion in this book:

- **Alvar Aalto/Artek** p142
- **John Anderson** p113
- **David Atkinson** p171
  www.atkinsonwoodart.com
- **Anthony Aylward** pp134, 154
  www.anthonyaylward.com
- **Fred Baier** pp146, 165
  www.fredbaier.com
- **Max Bainbridge** p162
  Forest + Found
  www.forest-and-found.com
- **David Barron** p171
  www.davidbarronfurniture.co.uk
- **Ian Birchall** p151
  www.urbancountrychair.com
- **Alice Blogg** p149
  www.aliceblogg.co.uk
- **Boddington & Foote** p89
  Special commission for Artizana
  by Silver Lining Workshops
- **Jeremy Broun**
  pp50, 144, 150, 161, 167
  www.jeremybroun.co.uk
- **Christopher Burley** pp140, 155
  www.heliconia-furniture.co.uk
- **Sally Burnett** p164
  www.sallyburnett.co.uk
  Photo: Simon Bruntnell, www.
  northlightphotographer.co.uk
- **Marcin Calka** p168
  www.rebornart.ie
- **Tom Cooper** pp134, 155, 156
  Tom Cooper Fine Furniture
  www.tcfinefurniture.co.uk
  Photo: Tina Sorensen
- **Deep Spring Studio/
  The Rosen Group** p66
- **John Eadon** p156
  www.johneadon.co.uk
  Photo: Nick Warner
  www.nickwarner.co.uk
- **Rob Elliot** p159
  www.robelliotfurniture.com
- **Joshua Gabriel** p158
  www.bengabriel.com

- **Namon Gaston** p151
  www.namongaston.com
  Photo: Stuart McClay
  www.stuartmcclay.com
- **Karen Hansen** pp145, 170
  Design & Natural Form
  www.karenhansen.co.uk
  Photo (p170): Iben Kaufman
- **Martin Harvey** pp135, 136, 171
  www.martinharveyfurniture.co.uk
- **Christopher Hauth** pp167, 168
- **Edward Hopkins** p89
- **Robert Ingham** p125
  www.robertinghamdesigns.com
- **Sarah Kay** pp130, 160
  www.sarah-kay.co.uk
- **Tobias Kaye** p143
  www.soundingbowls.com
- **Jeff Kemp** p169
- **Martin Lane** pp125
  www.martinlane.co.uk
  Photo: Blantern & Davis
- **Andrew Lapthorn** pp138, 161
  www.lapthornfurniture.co.uk
- **Andrew Lawton** pp137, 141
  www.andrewlawton.co.uk
  Photo: John Mottershaw
  www.johnmottershaw.com
- **Jonathan Leech** p163
  www.jonathanleech.co.uk
- **John Makepeace** pp139, 157
  www.johnmakepeace
  furniture.com
- **Christine Meyer-Eaglestone**
  pp132, 133, 164, 165
  www.cme-art.co.uk
- **Terrie Noll** p150
- **Alan Peters** pp73, 141, 154
  Courtesy of Mrs Alan Peters
- **Tony Portus** p136
  www.makerseye.co.uk
  Photo: Paul Lapsley
- **Tom Rauschke and
  Kaaren Wiken** p163
  Photo: William Lemke
- **Mark Ripley** pp135, 148
  www.mark-ripley.com
  Photo: Martin Phelps
- **Kevin Stamper** p159
  www.kevinstamperfurniture.com
- **Michael Thonet** p143
  Hescot Ltd, Newmarket
- **David Tragen** p158
  www.davidtragen.co.uk

- **Chris Tribe** pp132, 133, 160
  www.christribefurniture
  courses.com
- **Chris Turner** p140
  www.turnerfurniture.co.uk
  Photo: Paul T Cowan
  www.paultcowan.com
- **Andrew Varah** p137
- **Tom Vaughan** pp10, 146, Object
  Studio, www.objectstudio.co.uk
  Photo: Sam Barker
- **Nico Villeneuve** p138
  NICO, www.nicofurniture.com
- **Katie Walker** p147
  www.katiewalkerfurniture.com
- **Hans J. Wegner** pp143, 144
  Wegner/PP Mobler APS, Denmark
- **Thomas Whittingham**
  pp133, 148, 152, 153
  www.twfurniture.co.uk
- **Scott Woyka** pp6, 145, 149, 166
  www.scottwoyka.co.uk
- **Jolyon Yates** pp2, 147
  www.odechair.com

Special thanks to:
- **Axminster** for supplying images
  of tools, including: p8 (respirator
  & in-use photo), p23 (Proxxon/
  Wiha screwdrivers), p24 (cordless
  drill), p25 (jigsaw), p25 (router),
  p26 (circular saw), p27 (random
  orbital sander), p28 (chop/mitre
  saw), pp101 & 106 (Arbortech
  tool & in-use photos). All images
  courtesy of Axminster Tool
  Centre Ltd, Axminster Tools &
  Machinery, www.axminster.co.uk

Thanks also to:
- **AirPress Developments Ltd** p27
  (vacuum press) www.airpress.co.uk
- **Jeremy Broun** p17 (engineered
  veneers), p24 (screwdriver bits)
- **Power Adhesives** p111 (glue
  gun) www.poweradhesives.com
- **Trend Routing Technology** p8
  (half mask) www.trend-uk.com

Additional images supplied by:
www.shutterstock.com
pp4–5 Tomas Jasinskis;
p9 (dust mask) jocic; p19
(Japanese saw) donatas1205

All other photographs and illustrations are the copyright of Quarto Publishing plc. While every effort has been made to credit contributors, Quarto would like to apologise should there have been any omissions or errors – and would be pleased to make the appropriate correction for future editions of the book.

Special thanks to the following for the loan of tools and materials for photography and demonstrations:
- **Tools supplied by:** Axminster
  Tool Centre Ltd, AEG (UK) Ltd,
  Black & Decker, Bosch Power
  Tools, Franchi Lock & Tools,
  Hitachi (UK) Ltd, Kity, Luna Tools
  Ltd (Ryobi), Makita Power Tools,
  Panasonic Power Tools, Record
  Power Tools, Skil, Stanley Tools,
  Trend Cutting Tools, Wolfcraft.
- **Materials supplied by:** The Art
  Veneers Company Ltd, John
  Boddy Timber Ltd, Oscar
  Windebank Ltd, Silverman's
  and Sons Sheet Materials,
  Sp Systems – Isle of Wight.

We would like to acknowledge the following authors for their contributions to power and machine tools, sawing (track saw, chop/mitre saw), biscuit and domino joints, and vacuum press veneering:
- **Paul Forrester**
  Woodworker's Technique Bible
- **Chris Tribe**
  Complete Woodworking

Thanks also to:
- **Andrew Lawton** for technical
  assistance
- **Christine Meyer-Eaglestone** for
  supplying engineered veneers for
  photography and assistance with
  the Themes chapter